Contents

Lesson	Step	Sound	Main Alternative Vowel Spellings	Tricky Words	Letters and Sounds Phase	Page
1	3.1	i	i	once	5	5
2	3.1	i	y		5	6
Review 3	3.1	i	i, y		5	7
4	3.1	ai	ai	put	5	8
5	3.1	ai	a-e		5	9
6	3.1	ai	ay	push	5	10
7	3.1	ai	ey	pull	5	11
8	3.1	ai	a		5	12
Review 9	3.1	ai	ai, a-e, ay, ey, a		5	13
10	3.1	ee	ee		5	14
11	3.1	ee	ea	please	5	15
12	3.1	ee	e		5	16
13	3.1	ee	e-e		5	17
14	3.1	ee	y		5	18
15	3.1	ee	ie		5	19
Review 16	3.1	ee	ee, ea, e, e-e, y, ie		5	20
17	3.1	ie	ie	great	5	21
18	3.1	ie	i-e		5	22
19	3.1	ie	igh		5	23
20	3.1	ie	y		5	24
21	3.1	ie	i		5	25
Review 22	3.1	ie	ie, i-e, igh, y, i		5	26
23	3.1	oa	oa	eyes	5	27
24	3.1	oa	o-e		5	28
25	3.1	oa	o		5	29
26	3.1	oa	ow		5	30
27	3.1	oa	ou		5	31
Review 28	3.1	oa	oa, o-e, o, ow, ou		5	32
29	3.1	ue	ue	when	5	33
30	3.1	ue	u-e		5	34
31	3.1	ue	u		5	35
32	3.1	ue	ew		5	36
Review 33	3.1	ue	ue, u-e, u, ew		5	37
34	3.1	ar	ar	where	5	38

Contents

Lesson	Step	Sound	Main Alternative Vowel Spellings	Tricky Words	Letters and Sounds Phase	Page
35	3.1	ar	a		5	39
Review 36	3.1	ar	ar, a		5	40
37	3.1	er	er	though	5	41
38	3.1	er	ur		5	42
39	3.1	er	ir		5	43
Review 40	3.1	er	er, ur, ir		5	44
41	3.1	or	or		5	45
42	3.1	or	au	autumn	5	46
43	3.1	or	aw		5	47
44	3.1	or	al		5	48
Review 45	3.1	or	or, au, aw, al		5	49
46	3.1	oi	oi	again	5	50
47	3.1	oi	oy		5	51
Review 48	3.1	oi	oi, oy		5	52
49	3.1	ou	ou		5	53
50	3.1	ou	ow		5	54
Review 51	3.1	ou	ou, ow		5	55
52	3.1	oo	oo	I've	5	56
53	3.1	oo	oul		5	57
54	3.1	oo	u		5	58
Review 55	3.1	oo	oo, oul, u		5	59
56	3.1	oo	oo	what	5	60
57	3.1	oo	ue		5	61
58	3.1	oo	ew		5	62
59	3.1	oo	u-e		5	63
60	3.1	oo	ou		5	64
61	3.1	oo	o		5	65
Review 62	3.1	oo	oo, ue, ew, u-e, ou, o		5	66
63	3.1	e	e	their	5	67
64	3.1	e	ea		5	68
65	3.1	e	ai		5	69
66	3.1	e	ie		5	70
Review 67	3.1	e	e, ea, ai, ie		5	71
68	3.1	u	u	Mr, Mrs	5	72

Contents

Lesson	Step	Sound	Main Alternative Vowel Spellings	Tricky Words	Letters and Sounds Phase	Page
69	3.1	u	ou		5	73
70	3.1	u	o-e		5	74
71	3.1	u	o		5	75
Review 72	3.1	u	u, ou, o-e, o		5	76
73	3.2	c	c		5	77
74	3.2	c	k		5	78
75	3.2	c	ck		5	79
76	3.2	c	ch		5	80
Review 77	3.2	c	c, k, ck, ch		5	81
78	3.2	j	j	little	5	82
79	3.2	j	g(e)		5	83
80	3.2	j	g(i)		5	84
81	3.2	j	g(y)		5	85
82	3.2	j	ge		5	86
83	3.2	j	dge		5	87
Review 84	3.2	j	j, g(e), g(i), g(y), ge, dge		5	88
85	3.2	ch	ch	water	5	89
86	3.2	ch	tch		5	90
Review 87	3.2	ch	ch, tch		5	91
88	3.2	ng+k	nk	gone, goes	5	92
89	3.2	s	s		5	93
90	3.2	s	ss		5	94
91	3.2	s	c(e)		5	95
92	3.2	s	c(i)	circle	5	96
93	3.2	s	c(y)		5	97
94	3.2	s	ce		5	98
95	3.2	s	se		5	99
Review 96	3.2	s	s, ss, c(e), c(i), c(y), ce, se		5	100
97	3.2	w	w	people	5	101
98	3.2	w	wh		5	102
Review 99	3.2	w	w, wh		5	103
100	3.2	sh	ch		5	104
101	3.2	f	f		5	105

Contents

Lesson	Step	Sound	Main Alternative Vowel Spellings	Tricky Words	Letters and Sounds Phase	Page
102	3.2	f	ff		5	106
103	3.2	f	ph		5	107
104	3.2	f	gh	laugh, cough	5	108
Review 105	3.2	f	ff, ph, gh		5	109

Snappy Lesson 1

STEP 3.1

Sound /i/ written as i

Learning Objectives: to learn the main ways of spelling the sound /i/; to blend and segment words and sentences containing i

Success Criteria: to read words and sentences containing i spelling of sound /i/ and write dictated words and sentences with 100% accuracy

Reading	Spelling
1. Review Sounds (show as pack) • s a t p i n	**8. Sounds Write** • s a t p i n
2. Spelling: i Show the flashcard for **i**. Then with all the phonemes play the **Grab Game**. With the cards on the table, say a sound and ask the children to 'grab' for the letter. **Fingertips Freeze** when they touch the flashcard. Only allow one 'grab'.	**9. Spelling: i** Model writing the letter on the board and talk through letter formation. **Sky Write** the letter together. Ask children to write the sound on their whiteboards or paper. Check the letter formation for the correct start point, exit stroke and place on the line.
3. Oral Blending (Robot Game) Play the **Robot Game**. Pretend to be a Robot who can only speak in sounds (robot speech), moving arms back and forth like robot arms, in time with each sound. • Say the sounds **h-i-t**, ask children to listen and say the word**.** • Repeat for: **milk, drip, twist**	**10. Oral Segmenting (Phoneme Fingers)** Say a word and the children use **Phoneme Fingers** to flick their fingers for each sound in: • h-i-t, m-i-l-k, d-r-i-p, t-w-i-s-t

4. Manipulating (Swap) Sounds

Stick vowel cards at the top of the board: **a i**. Stick consonant cards at the bottom: **b d h t**

Play the **Full Circle Word Game** using the letters on the board to make a word. Ask the children to use **Phoneme Fingers** for each sound in the word. Read the word to the children. Ask a child to change one or more sounds in the word, swapping card/s from the word with card/s at either the bottom or the top of the board. Use **Phoneme Fingers** to make and read the new word. Continue the game changing one sound at a time until you get back to the first word made.

Full circle words: bit, bid, hid, had, bad, bat, bit

5. Reading Words Ask children to read these words: • hit, milk, drip, twist	**11. Word Dictation** Ask children to tap for the sounds and write: • hit, milk, drip, twist
6. Reading Tricky Words: <u>once</u> • Show flashcard with the tricky bits underlined. • Together, with the children, sound and say the word using the known letter/sound matches. • Point out that the word doesn't sound like this, identify the tricky bits, and provide tricky sounds: the 'o' sounds /wu/ and the 'ce' sound /s/. • Sound and say the word correctly together.	**12. Tricky Words Dictation: <u>once</u>** • Say the tricky word and remind children to watch out for the tricky bits. • Ask children to say the word, tap for the sounds and write each grapheme. Model with **Phoneme Fingers**, if necessary.
7. Reading Sentences (See page 110) He hit the nail with his hammer. She had a cup of milk. The tap has a drip. You twist the jar once.	**13. Sentence Dictation** (See page 110) He hit the nail with his hammer. She had a cup of milk. The tap has a drip. You twist the jar once. After writing, children read back sounds, words and sentences.

Snappy Lesson 2

STEP 3.1

Sound /i/ written as y

Learning Objectives: to learn the main ways of spelling the sound /i/; to blend and segment words and sentences containing y

Success Criteria: to read words and sentences containing y spelling of sound /i/ and write dictated words and sentences with 100% accuracy

Reading	Spelling
1. Review Sounds (show as pack) • c e h r m d i	**7. Write Sounds** • c e h r m d i
2. New Spelling: y Show the flashcard for **y**. Then with all the phonemes play the **Grab Game**. With the cards on the table, say a sound and ask the children to 'grab' for the letter. **Fingertips Freeze** when they touch the flashcard. Only allow one 'grab'.	**8. New Spelling: y** Model writing the letter on the board and talk through letter formation. **Sky Write** the letter together. Ask children to write the sound on their whiteboards or paper. Check the letter formation for the correct start point, exit stroke and place on the line.
3. Oral Blending (Robot Game) Play the **Robot Game**. Pretend to be a Robot who can only speak in sounds (robot speech), moving arms back and forth like robot arms, in time with each sound. • Say the sounds **p-y-r-a-m-i-d**, ask children to listen and say the word. • Repeat for: **myth, sympathetic, Olympics**	**9. Oral Segmenting (Phoneme Fingers)** Say a word and the children use **Phoneme Fingers** to flick their fingers for each sound in: • p-y-r-a-m-i-d, m-y-th, s-y-m-p-a-th-e-t-i-c, O-l-y-m-p-i-c-s

4. Manipulating (Swap) Sounds

Stick vowel cards at the top of the board: **o u a y** (/i/ vowel sound)

Stick consonant cards at the bottom: **h m m th p**

Play the **Full Circle Word Game** using the letters on the board to make a word. Ask the children to use **Phoneme Fingers** for each sound in the word. Read the word to the children. Ask a child to change one or more sounds in the word, swapping card/s from the word with card/s at either the bottom or the top of the board. Use **Phoneme Fingers** to make and read the new word. Continue the game changing one sound at a time until you get back to the first word made.

Full circle words: moth, myth, mum, hum, ham, path, moth

5. Reading Words Ask children to read these words: • **pyramid, myth, sympathetic, Olympics**	**10. Word Dictation** Ask children to tap for the sounds and write: • **pyramid, myth, sympathetic, Olympics**
6. Reading Sentences (See page 110) We visited the pyramids. Atlantis is a myth. The card was sympathetic. The sprinter went to the Olympics.	**11. Sentence Dictation** (See page 110) We visited the pyramids. Atlantis is a myth. The card was sympathetic. The sprinter went to the Olympics. After writing, children read back sounds, words and sentences.

Snappy Lesson 3 — FastTrack

STEP 3.1

Review: Sound /i/ written as i, y

Learning Objectives: to review a set of letter/sound correspondences; to learn the main ways of spelling the sound /i/, read these spelling choices in words and sentences and write them in dictated words and sentences.

Example grid:

i	y
pin	myth
sit	crystal
limp	sympathetic
wind	pyramid
slip	Olympics
wish	

1. Draw a blank two-column grid on the board and explain that the group will be finding the main ways that the sound /i/ can be written down.

2. Show the flashcard for /i/ and ask children the main ways of writing the /i/ sound. They may use letter names. Write the graphemes at the top of the columns on the grid.

3. Ask the children to say a word that contains the sound /i/ and then to say which column it goes into. Write the choice in the correct column.

4. Ask the children to continue to generate examples while you write them in the correct column. There are some examples shown in the grid above if the children need prompting. Keep going until the columns are full.

5. Ask one child to come to the board, read the words in that column, underline the pattern, and comment on the position of the alternative spelling pattern in the word (i.e. beginning, middle or end).

6. Ask children to come to the board in turn until all of the alternative spelling patterns have been read, underlined and the position of the alternative spelling pattern commented on.

7. Children copy the grid into their books. Explain that they can add to this over time. Alternatively, make copies of the grid (see page 110) and stick these into the children's books. Explain that the words in this grid may not be exactly the same as those the children came up with.

8. Remove the grid from the board and dictate words (see example grid above) and the following sentences to the group for them to write down on a clean page or mini-whiteboard.

   The man has a bad limp.
   Dragons are a myth.

9. After writing the dictation, ask the children to read back a selection of words and sentences. Check for correct spelling choices and punctuation.

10. Ask the children to write a sentence of their own, using one of the words they have encountered. Listen to the children say the sentences aloud first. Moderate grammar and check for correct spelling choices and punctuation.

Snappy Lesson 4

STEP 3.1

Sound /ai/ written as ai

Learning Objectives: to learn the main ways of spelling the sound /ai/; to blend and segment words and sentences containing ai

Success Criteria: to read words and sentences containing ai spelling of sound /ai/ and write dictated words and sentences with 100% accuracy

Reading	Spelling
1. Review Sounds (show as pack) • g o u l f b i y	**8. Write Sounds** • g o u l f b i y
2. Spelling: ai Show the flashcard for **ai**. Then with all the phonemes play the **Grab Game**. With the cards on the table, say a sound and ask the children to 'grab' for the letter. **Fingertips Freeze** when they touch the flashcard. Only allow one 'grab'.	**9. Spelling: ai** Model writing the letters on the board and talk through letter formation from exit stroke of first letter to start point of the next letter for joined-up writing. **Sky Write** the letters together. Ask children to write the sound on their whiteboards or paper. Check the letter formation for the correct start points, exit strokes and place on the line.
3. Oral Blending (Robot Game) Play the **Robot Game**. Pretend to be a Robot who can only speak in sounds (robot speech), moving arms back and forth like robot arms, in time with each sound. • Say the sounds **p-ai-n**, ask children to listen and say the word. • Repeat for: **aim, sail, stain**	**10. Oral Segmenting (Phoneme Fingers)** Say a word and the children use **Phoneme Fingers** to flick their fingers for each sound in: • **p-ai-n, ai-m, s-ai-l, s-t-ai-n**

4. Manipulating (Swap) Sounds

Stick vowel cards at the top of the board: **a ai**. Stick consonant cards at the bottom: **b l p t**

Play the **Full Circle Word Game** using the letters on the board to make a word. Ask the children to use **Phoneme Fingers** for each sound in the word. Read the word to the children. Ask a child to change one or more sounds in the word, swapping card/s from the word with card/s at either the bottom or the top of the board. Use **Phoneme Fingers** to make and read the new word. Continue the game changing one sound at a time until you get back to the first word made.

Full circle words: bat, bait, bail, pail, pal, pat, bat

5. Reading Words Ask children to read these words: • **pain, aim, sail, stain**	**11. Word Dictation** Ask children to tap for the sounds and write: • **pain, aim, sail, stain**
6. Reading Tricky Words: p<u>u</u>t • Show flashcard with the tricky bit underlined. • Together, with the children, sound and say the word using the known letter/sound matches. • Point out that the word doesn't sound like this, identify the tricky bit, and provide tricky sound : the 'u' makes the short /oo/ sound. • Sound and say the word correctly together.	**12. Tricky Words Dictation: p<u>u</u>t** • Say the tricky word and remind children to watch out for the tricky bit. • Ask children to say the word, tap for the sounds and write each grapheme. Model with **Phoneme Fingers**, if necessary.
7. Reading Sentences (See page 111) She put a nail in the pail. I shall aim at the target. Can the boat sail to Scotland? There was a stain on the carpet.	**13. Sentence Dictation** (See page 111) She put a nail in the pail. I shall aim at the target. Can the boat sail to Scotland? There was a stain on the carpet. After writing, children read back sounds, words and sentences.

Snappy Lesson 5

STEP 3.1

Sound /ai/ written as a-e

Learning Objectives: to learn the main ways of spelling the sound /ai/; to blend and segment words and sentences containing a-e

Success Criteria: to read words and sentences containing a-e spelling of sound /ai/ and write dictated words and sentences with 100% accuracy

Reading	Spelling
1. Review Sounds (show as pack) • j v w z y i y (/i/ vowel sound) ai	**7. Write Sounds** • j v w z y i y (/i/ vowel sound) ai
2. New Spelling: a-e Show the flashcard for **a-e**. Then with all the phonemes play the **Grab Game**. With the cards on the table, say a sound and ask the children to 'grab' for the letter. **Fingertips Freeze** when they touch the flashcard. Only allow one 'grab'.	**8. New Spelling: a-e** Model writing the letters on the board and talk through letter formations. **Sky Write** the letters together. Ask children to write the sound on their whiteboards or paper. Check the letter formations for the correct start points, exit strokes and place on the line.
3. Oral Blending (Robot Game) Play the **Robot Game**. Pretend to be a Robot who can only speak in sounds (robot speech), moving arms back and forth like robot arms, in time with each sound. • Say the sounds **d-(a-e)-t**, ask children to listen and say the word. • Repeat for: **cake, lane, game**	**9. Oral Segmenting (Phoneme Fingers)** Say a word and the children use **Phoneme Fingers** to flick their fingers for each sound in: • d-(a-e)-t, c-(a-e)-k, l-(a-e)-n, g-(a-e)-m

4. Manipulating (Swap) Sounds

Stick vowel cards at the top of the board: **a e ai a-e**. Stick consonant cards at the bottom: **b g m t**

Play the **Full Circle Word Game** using the letters on the board to make a word. Use two separate cards to make the split digraph a-e, ensuring children understand that this makes one sound. Ask the children to use **Phoneme Fingers** for each sound in the word. Read the word to the children. Ask a child to change one or more sounds in the word, swapping card/s from the word with card/s at either the bottom or the top of the board. Use **Phoneme Fingers** to make and read the new word. Continue the game changing one sound at a time until you get back to the first word made.

Full circle words: at, ate, gate, gait, bait, bet, met, mate, ate, at

| **5. Reading Words**
Ask children to read these words:
• date, cake, lane, game | **10. Word Dictation**
Ask children to tap for the sounds and write:
• date, cake, lane, game |
| **6. Reading Sentences** (See page 111)
Josh went on a date with Liz.
She put the cake in a tin.
The car got stuck in the lane.
We had a good game of tennis. | **11. Sentence Dictation** (See page 111)
Josh went on a date with Liz.
She put the cake in a tin.
The car got stuck in the lane.
We had a good game of tennis.

After writing, children read back sounds, words and sentences. |

Look out for tricky word: put

Snappy Lesson 6

STEP 3.1

Sound /ai/ written as ay

Learning Objectives: to learn the main ways of spelling the sound /ai/; to blend and segment words and sentences containing ay

Success Criteria: to read words and sentences containing ay spelling of sound /ai/ and write dictated words and sentences with 100% accuracy

Reading	Spelling
1. Review Sounds (show as pack) • k qu x i y ai a-e	**8. Write Sounds** • k qu x i y ai a-e
2. New Spelling: ay Show the flashcard for **ay**. Then with all the phonemes play the **Grab Game**. With the cards on the table, say a sound and ask the children to 'grab' for the letter. **Fingertips Freeze** when they touch the flashcard. Only allow one 'grab'.	**9. New Spelling: ay** Model writing the letters on the board and talk through letter formation from exit stroke of first letter to start point of the next letter for joined-up writing. **Sky Write** the letters together. Ask children to write the sound on their whiteboards or paper. Check the letter formation for the correct start points, exit strokes and place on the line.
3. Oral Blending (Robot Game) Play the **Robot Game**. Pretend to be a Robot who can only speak in sounds (robot speech), moving arms back and forth like robot arms, in time with each sound. • Say the sounds **h-ay**, ask children to listen and say the word. • Repeat for: **lay, stray, pray**	**10. Oral Segmenting (Phoneme Fingers)** Say a word and the children use **Phoneme Fingers** to flick their fingers for each sound in: • h-ay, l-ay, s-t-r-ay, p-r-ay

4. Manipulating (Swap) Sounds

Stick vowel cards at the top of the board: **a ai a-e ay**. Stick consonant cards at the bottom: **d l m p r**

Play the **Full Circle Word Game** using the letters on the board to make a word. Use two separate cards to make the split digraph a-e, ensuring children understand that this makes one sound. Ask the children to use **Phoneme Fingers** for each sound in the word. Read the word to the children. Ask a child to change one or more sounds in the word, swapping card/s from the word with card/s at either the bottom or the top of the board. Use **Phoneme Fingers** to make and read the new word. Continue the game changing one sound at a time until you get back to the first word made.

Full circle words: ray, rail, maid, made, mad, pad, paid, pay, ray

5. Reading Words Ask children to read these words: • hay, lay, stray, pray	**11. Word Dictation** Ask children to tap for the sounds and write: • hay, lay, stray, pray
6. Reading Tricky Words: p<u>u</u>sh • Show flashcard with the tricky bit underlined. • Together, with the children, sound and say the word using the known letter/sound matches. • Point out that the word doesn't sound like this, identify the tricky bit, and provide tricky sound: the 'u' makes the short /oo/ sound. • Sound and say the word correctly together.	**12. Tricky Words Dictation: p<u>u</u>sh** • Say the tricky word and remind children to watch out for the tricky bit. • Ask children to say the word, tap for the sounds and write each grapheme. Model with **Phoneme Fingers**, if necessary.
7. Reading Sentences (See page 111) Push the hay into the pen. The coins lay deep in the soil. He fed the stray cat. We will pray at school.	**13. Sentence Dictation** (See page 111) Push the hay into the pen. The coins lay deep in the soil. He fed the stray cat. We will pray at school. After writing, children read back sounds, words and sentences.

Snappy Lesson 7

STEP 3.1

Sound /ai/ written as ey

Learning Objectives: to learn the main ways of spelling the sound /ai/; to blend and segment words and sentences containing ey

Success Criteria: to read words and sentences containing ey spelling of sound /ai/ and write dictated words and sentences with 100% accuracy

Reading	Spelling
1. Review Sounds (show as pack) • sh ch th ng i y ai a-e ay	**8. Write Sounds** • sh ch th ng i y ai a-e ay
2. New Spelling: ey Show the flashcard for **ey**. Then with all the phonemes play the **Grab Game**. With the cards on the table, say a sound and ask the children to 'grab' for the letter. **Fingertips Freeze** when they touch the flashcard. Only allow one 'grab'.	**9. New Spelling: ey** Model writing the letters on the board and talk through letter formation from exit stroke of first letter to start point of the next letter for joined-up writing. **Sky Write** the letters together. Ask children to write the sound on their whiteboards or paper. Check the letter formation for the correct start points, exit strokes and place on the line.
3. Oral Blending (Robot Game) Play the **Robot Game**. Pretend to be a Robot who can only speak in sounds (robot speech), moving arms back and forth like robot arms, in time with each sound. • Say the sounds **p-r-ey**, ask children to listen and say the word. • Repeat for: **they, grey, obey**	**10. Oral Segmenting (Phoneme Fingers)** Say a word and the children use **Phoneme Fingers** to flick their fingers for each sound in: • **p-r-ey, th-e-y, g-r-ey, o-b-ey**

4. Manipulating (Swap) Sounds

Stick vowel cards at the top of the board: **a-e ay ey**. Stick consonant cards at the bottom: **g l p r t**

Play the **Full Circle Word Game** using the letters on the board to make a word. Ask the children to use **Phoneme Fingers** for each sound in the word. Read the word to the children. Use two separate cards to make the split digraph a-e, ensuring children understand that this makes one sound. Ask a child to change one or more sounds in the word, swapping card/s from the word with card/s at either the bottom or the top of the board. Use **Phoneme Fingers** to make and read the new word. Continue the game changing one sound at a time until you get back to the first word made.

Full circle words: prey, pray, play, lay, late, gate, grate, grey, prey

5. Reading Words Ask children to read these words: • prey, they, grey, obey	**11. Word Dictation** Ask children to tap for the sounds and write: • prey, they, grey, obey
6. Reading Tricky Words: pu̲ll • Show flashcard with the tricky bit underlined. • Together, with the children, sound and say the word using the known letter/sound matches. • Point out that the word doesn't sound like this, identify the tricky bit, and provide tricky sound: the 'u' makes the short /oo/ sound. • Sound and say the word correctly together.	**12. Tricky Words Dictation: pu̲ll** • Say the tricky word and remind children to watch out for the tricky bit. • Ask children to say the word, tap for the sounds and write each grapheme. Model with **Phoneme Fingers**, if necessary.
7. Reading Sentences (See page 112) The shark ate its prey. They had to pull on the chain. Her coat was grey with a red trim. I will obey my mum.	**13. Sentence Dictation** (See page 112) The shark ate its prey. They had to pull on the chain. Her coat was grey with a red trim. I will obey my mum. After writing, children read back sounds, words and sentences.

Snappy Lesson 8

STEP 3.1

Sound /ai/ written as a

Learning Objectives: to learn the main ways of spelling the sound /ai/; to blend and segment words and sentences containing a

Success Criteria: to read words and sentences containing a spelling of sound /ai/ and write dictated words and sentences with 100% accuracy

Reading

1. Review Sounds (show as pack)
- ai ee ie oa ue i y ai a-e ay ey

2. New Spelling: a

Show the flashcard for **a**. Then with all the phonemes play the **Grab Game**. With the cards on the table, say a sound and ask the children to 'grab' for the letter. **Fingertips Freeze** when they touch the flashcard. Only allow one 'grab'.

3. Oral Blending (Robot Game)

Play the **Robot Game**. Pretend to be a Robot who can only speak in sounds (robot speech), moving arms back and forth like robot arms, in time with each sound.
- Say the sounds **b-a-b-y**, ask children to listen and say the word.
- Repeat for: **April, vacant, paper**

4. Manipulating (Swap) Sounds

Stick vowel cards at the top of the board: **y ai a-e ay a**
Stick consonant cards at the bottom: **d g l n p r t**

Play the **Full Circle Word Game** using the letters on the board to make a word. Use two separate cards to make the split digraph a-e, ensuring children understand that this makes one sound. Ask the children to use **Phoneme Fingers** for each sound in the word. Read the word to the children. Ask a child to change one or more sounds in the word, swapping card/s from the word with card/s at either the bottom or the top of the board. Use **Phoneme Fingers** to make and read the new word. Continue the game changing one sound at a time until you get back to the first word made.

Full circle words: gate, gain, pay, pray, lay, lady, laid, late, gate

5. Reading Words

Ask children to read these words:
- baby, April, vacant, paper

6. Reading Sentences (See page 112)

The baby slept in his pram.
The spring bulbs came up in April.
Is the house vacant?
Did the paper bag split?

Spelling

7. Write Sounds
- ai ee ie oa ue i y ai a-e ay ey

8. New Spelling: a

Model writing the letter on the board and talk through letter formation. **Sky Write** the letter together. Ask children to write the sound on their whiteboards or paper. Check the letter formation for the correct start point, exit stroke and place on the line.

9. Oral Segmenting (Phoneme Fingers)

Say a word and the children use **Phoneme Fingers** to flick their fingers for each sound in:
- b-a-b-y, A-p-r-i-l, v-a-c-a-n-t, p-a-p-er

10. Word Dictation

Ask children to tap for the sounds and write:
- baby, April, vacant, paper

11. Sentence Dictation (See page 112)

The baby slept in his pram.
The spring bulbs came up in April.
Is the house vacant?
Did the paper bag split?

After writing, children read back sounds, words and sentences.

Snappy Lesson 9 *FastTrack*

STEP 3.1

Review: Sound /ai/ written as ai, a-e, ay, ey, a

Learning Objectives: to review a set of letter/sound correspondences; to learn the main ways of spelling the sound /ai/, read these spelling choices in words and sentences and write them in dictated words and sentences.

Example grid:

ai	a-e	ay	ey	a
rain	made	day	they	paper
main	came	say	grey	acorn
rail	make	may	prey	bacon
wait	late	lay	obey	bagel
train	same	play		apricot
snail	snake	clay		

1. Draw a blank five-column grid on the board and explain that the group will be finding the main ways that the sound /ai/ can be written down.

2. Show the flashcard for /ai/ and ask children the main ways of writing the /ai/ sound. They may use letter names. Write the graphemes at the top of the columns on the grid.

3. Ask the children to say a word that contains the sound /ai/ and then to say which column it goes into. Write the choice in the correct column.

4. Ask the children to continue to generate examples while you write them in the correct column. There are some examples shown in the grid above if the children need prompting. Keep going until the columns are full.

5. Ask one child to come to the board, read the words in that column, underline the pattern, and comment on the position of the alternative spelling pattern in the word (i.e. beginning, middle or end).

6. Ask children to come to the board in turn until all of the aternative spelling patterns have been read, underlined and the position of the alternative spelling pattern commented on.

7. Children copy the grid into their books. Explain that they can add to this over time. Alternatively, make copies of the grid (see page 112) and stick these into the children's books. Explain that the words in this grid may not be exactly the same as those the children came up with.

8. Remove the grid from the board and dictate words (see example grid above) and the following sentences to the group for them to write down on a clean page or mini-whiteboard.

   We must wait in the rain.
   I can bake a cake.
   Tom went on a day trip.
   They must obey the king.
   Liz had apricot jam.

9. After writing the dictation, ask the children to read back a selection of words and sentences. Check for correct spelling choices and punctuation.

10. Ask the children to write a sentence of their own, using one of the words they have encountered. Listen to the children say the sentences aloud first. Moderate grammar and check for correct spelling choices and punctuation.

Snappy Lesson 10

STEP 3.1

Sound /ee/ written as ee

Learning Objectives: to learn the main ways of spelling the sound /ee/; to blend and segment words and sentences containing ee

Success Criteria: to read words and sentences containing ee spelling of sound /ee/ and write dictated words and sentences with 100% accuracy

Reading	Spelling
1. Review Sounds (show as pack) • ar er or ai a-e ay ey a	**7. Write Sounds** • ar er or ai a-e ay ey a
2. Spelling: ee Show the flashcard for **ee**. Then with all the phonemes play the **Grab Game**. With the cards on the table, say a sound and ask the children to 'grab' for the letter. **Fingertips Freeze** when they touch the flashcard. Only allow one 'grab'.	**8. Spelling: ee** Model writing the letters on the board and talk through letter formation from exit stroke of first letter to start point of the next letter for joined-up writing. **Sky Write** the letters together. Ask children to write the sound on their whiteboards or paper. Check the letter formation for the correct start points, exit strokes and place on the line.
3. Oral Blending (Robot Game) Play the **Robot Game**. Pretend to be a Robot who can only speak in sounds (robot speech), moving arms back and forth like robot arms, in time with each sound. • Say the sounds **k-ee-p**, ask children to listen and say the word. • Repeat for: **bee, meet, week**	**9. Oral Segmenting (Phoneme Fingers)** Say a word and the children use **Phoneme Fingers** to flick their fingers for each sound in: • **k-ee-p, b-ee, m-ee-t, w-ee-k**

4. Manipulating (Swap) Sounds

Stick vowel cards at the top of the board: **ee**. Stick consonant cards at the bottom: **b d f l n s**

Play the **Full Circle Word Game** using the letters on the board to make a word. Ask the children to use **Phoneme Fingers** for each sound in the word. Read the word to the children. Ask a child to change one or more sounds in the word, swapping card/s from the word with card/s at either the bottom or the top of the board. Use **Phoneme Fingers** to make and read the new word. Continue the game changing one sound at a time until you get back to the first word made.

Full circle words: bee, see, seed, need, feed, feel, fee, bee

5. Reading Words Ask children to read these words: • **keep, bee, meet, week**	**10. Word Dictation** Ask children to tap for the sounds and write: • **keep, bee, meet, week**
6. Reading Sentences (See page 113) **Keep her safe from harm.** **The bee stung me on the hand.** **Come and meet his sister.** **There are seven days in a week.**	**11. Sentence Dictation** (See page 113) **Keep her safe from harm.** **The bee stung me on the hand.** **Come and meet his sister.** **There are seven days in a week.** After writing, children read back sounds, words and sentences.

Snappy Lesson 11

STEP 3.1

Sound /ee/ written as ea

Learning Objectives: to learn the main ways of spelling the sound /ee/; to blend and segment words and sentences containing ea

Success Criteria: to read words and sentences containing ea spelling of sound /ee/ and write dictated words and sentences with 100% accuracy

Reading	Spelling
1. Review Sounds (show as pack) • oi ou oo **oo** ai a-e ay ey a ee	**8. Write Sounds** • oi ou oo **oo** ai a-e ay ey a ee
2. New Spelling: ea Show the flashcard for **ea**. Then with all the phonemes play the **Grab Game**. With the cards on the table, say a sound and ask the children to 'grab' for the letter. **Fingertips Freeze** when they touch the flashcard. Only allow one 'grab'.	**9. New Spelling: ea** Model writing the letters on the board and talk through letter formation from exit stroke of first letter to start point of the next letter for joined-up writing. **Sky Write** the letters together. Ask children to write the sound on their whiteboards or paper. Check the letter formation for the correct start points, exit strokes and place on the line.
3. Oral Blending (Robot Game) Play the **Robot Game**. Pretend to be a Robot who can only speak in sounds (robot speech), moving arms back and forth like robot arms, in time with each sound. • Say the sounds **s-ea-t**, ask children to listen and say the word. • Repeat for: **leaf, treat, least**	**10. Oral Segmenting (Phoneme Fingers)** Say a word and the children use **Phoneme Fingers** to flick their fingers for each sound in: • **s-ea-t, l-ea-f, t-r-ea-t, l-ea-s-t**
4. Manipulating (Swap) Sounds Stick vowel cards at the top of the board: **ee ea**. Stick consonant cards at the bottom: **b s t ch** Play the **Full Circle Word Game** using the letters on the board to make a word. Ask the children to use **Phoneme Fingers** for each sound in the word. Read the word to the children. Ask a child to change one or more sounds in the word, swapping card/s from the word with card/s at either the bottom or the top of the board. Use **Phoneme Fingers** to make and read the new word. Continue the game changing one sound at a time until you get back to the first word made. **Full circle words: eat, seat, sea, see, tee, tea, teach, each, beach, beat, eat**	
5. Reading Words Ask children to read these words: • **seat, leaf, treat, least**	**11. Word Dictation** Ask children to tap for the sounds and write: • **seat, leaf, treat, least**
6. Reading Tricky Words: plea<u>se</u> • Show flashcard with the tricky bit underlined. • Together, with the children, sound and say the word using the known letter/sound matches. • Point out that the word doesn't sound like this, identify the tricky bit, and provide tricky sound: the 'se' sounds /z/. • Sound and say the word correctly together.	**12. Tricky Words Dictation: plea<u>se</u>** • Say the tricky word and remind children to watch out for the tricky bit. • Ask children to say the word, tap for the sounds and write each grapheme. Model with **Phoneme Fingers**, if necessary.
7. Reading Sentences (See page 113) **Please keep her safe from harm.** **Take a seat in the waiting room.** **A leaf fell from the tree.** **A cup of tea is such a treat.**	**13. Sentence Dictation** (See page 113) **Please keep her safe from harm.** **Take a seat in the waiting room.** **A leaf fell from the tree.** **A cup of tea is such a treat.** After writing, children read back sounds, words and sentences.

Snappy Lesson 12

STEP 3.1

Sound /ee/ written as e

Learning Objectives: to learn the main ways of spelling the sound /ee/; to blend and segment words and sentences containing e

Success Criteria: to read words and sentences containing e spelling of sound /ee/ and write dictated words and sentences with 100% accuracy

Reading	Spelling
1. Review Sounds (show as pack) • ai a-e ay ey a ee ea	**7. Write Sounds** • ai a-e ay ey a ee ea
2. New Spelling: e Show the flashcard for **e**. Then with all the phonemes play the **Grab Game**. With the cards on the table, say a sound and ask the children to 'grab' for the letter. **Fingertips Freeze** when they touch the flashcard. Only allow one 'grab'.	**8. New Spelling: e** Model writing the letter on the board and talk through letter formation. **Sky Write** the letter together. Ask children to write the sound on their whiteboards or paper. Check the letter formation for the correct start point, exit stroke and place on the line.
3. Oral Blending (Robot Game) Play the **Robot Game**. Pretend to be a Robot who can only speak in sounds (robot speech), moving arms back and forth like robot arms, in time with each sound. • Say the sounds **m-e**, ask children to listen and say the word. • Repeat for: **be**, **he, she**	**9. Oral Segmenting (Phoneme Fingers)** Say a word and the children use **Phoneme Fingers** to flick their fingers for each sound in: • **m-e, b-e, h-e, sh-e**

4. Manipulating (Swap) Sounds

Stick vowel cards at the top of the board: **ee ea e**. Stick consonant cards at the bottom: **b f m t sh**

Play the **Full Circle Word Game** using the letters on the board to make a word. Ask the children to use **Phoneme Fingers** for each sound in the word. Read the word to the children. Ask a child to change one or more sounds in the word, swapping card/s from the word with card/s at either the bottom or the top of the board. Use **Phoneme Fingers** to make and read the new word. Continue the game changing one sound at a time until you get back to the first word made.

Full circle words: me, be, bee, beef, beet, beat, meat, meet, sheet, she, me

5. Reading Words Ask children to read these words: • **me, be, he, she**	**10. Word Dictation** Ask children to tap for the sounds and write: • **me, be, he, she**
6. Reading Sentences (See page 113) They let me win. Will the lemon tart be hot? Did he go fishing? Can she visit her children?	**11. Sentence Dictation** (See page 113) They let me win. Will the lemon tart be hot? Did he go fishing? Can she visit her children? After writing, children read back sounds, words and sentences.

Snappy Lesson 13

STEP 3.1

Sound /ee/ written as e-e

Learning Objectives: to learn the main ways of spelling the sound /ee/; to blend and segment words and sentences containing e-e

Success Criteria: to read words and sentences containing e-e spelling of sound /ee/ and write dictated words and sentences with 100% accuracy

Reading	Spelling
1. Review Sounds (show as pack) • ai a-e ay ey a ee ea e	**7. Write Sounds** • ai a-e ay ey a ee ea e
2. New Spelling: e-e Show the flashcard for **e-e**. Then with all the phonemes play the **Grab Game**. With the cards on the table, say a sound and ask the children to 'grab' for the letter. **Fingertips Freeze** when they touch the flashcard. Only allow one 'grab'.	**8. New Spelling: e-e** Model writing the letters on the board and talk through letter formations. **Sky Write** the letters together. Ask children to write the sound on their whiteboards or paper. Check the letter formations for the correct start points, exit strokes and place on the line.
3. Oral Blending (Robot Game) Play the **Robot Game**. Pretend to be a Robot who can only speak in sounds (robot speech), moving arms back and forth like robot arms, in time with each sound. • Say the sounds **th-(e-e)-m**, ask children to listen and say the word. • Repeat for: **these, complete, extreme**	**9. Oral Segmenting (Phoneme Fingers)** Say a word and the children use **Phoneme Fingers** to flick their fingers for each sound in: • **th-(e-e)-m, th-(e-e)-s, c-o-m-p-l-(e-e)-t, e-x-t-r-(e-e)-m**

4. Manipulating (Swap) Sounds

Stick vowel cards at the top of the board: **i e e-e**. Stick consonant cards at the bottom: **h m s th**

Play the **Full Circle Word Game** using the letters on the board to make a word. Use two separate cards to make the split digraph e-e, ensuring children understand that this makes one sound. Ask the children to use **Phoneme Fingers** for each sound in the word. Read the word to the children. Ask a child to change one or more sounds in the word, swapping card/s from the word with card/s at either the bottom or the top of the board. Use **Phoneme Fingers** to make and read the new word. Continue the game changing one sound at a time until you get back to the first word made.

Full circle words: them, theme, these, this, his, him, them

5. Reading Words Ask children to read these words: • **theme, these, complete, extreme**	**10. Word Dictation** Ask children to tap for the sounds and write: • **theme, these, complete, extreme**
6. Reading Sentences (See page 114) **They visited a theme park.** **Will you help me pack these things?** **I need to complete the test.** **You must avoid extreme heat.**	**11. Sentence Dictation** (See page 114) **They visited a theme park.** **Will you help me pack these things?** **I need to complete the test.** **You must avoid extreme heat.** After writing, children read back sounds, words and sentences.

Snappy Lesson 14

STEP 3.1

Sound /ee/ written as y

Learning Objectives: to learn the main ways of spelling the sound /ee/; to blend and segment words and sentences containing y

Success Criteria: to read words and sentences containing y spelling of sound /ee/ and write dictated words and sentences with 100% accuracy

Reading	Spelling
1. Review Sounds (show as pack) • ai a-e ay ey a ee ea e e-e	**7. Write Sounds** • ai a-e ay ey a ee ea e e-e
2. New Spelling: y Show the flashcard for **y**. Then with all the phonemes play the **Grab Game**. With the cards on the table, say a sound and ask the children to 'grab' for the letter. **Fingertips Freeze** when they touch the flashcard. Only allow one 'grab'.	**8. New Spelling: y** Model writing the letter on the board and talk through letter formation. **Sky Write** the letter together. Ask children to write the sound on their whiteboards or paper. Check the letter formation for the correct start point, exit stroke and place on the line.
3. Oral Blending (Robot Game) Play the **Robot Game**. Pretend to be a Robot who can only speak in sounds (robot speech), moving arms back and forth like robot arms, in time with each sound. • Say the sounds **b-o-d-y**, ask children to listen and say the word. • Repeat for: **happy, mystery, sympathy**	**9. Oral Segmenting (Phoneme Fingers)** Say a word and the children use **Phoneme Fingers** to flick their fingers for each sound in: **b-o-d-y, h-a-p/p-y, m-y-s-t-e-r-y, s-y-m-p-a-th-y**

4. Manipulating (Swap) Sounds

Stick vowel cards at the top of the board: **a ar y**. Stick consonant cards at the bottom: **d h m n p p t**

Play the **Full Circle Word Game** using the letters on the board to make a word. Ask the children to use **Phoneme Fingers** for each sound in the word. Read the word to the children. Ask a child to change one or more sounds in the word, swapping card/s from the word with card/s at either the bottom or the top of the board. Use **Phoneme Fingers** to make and read the new word. Continue the game changing one sound at a time until you get back to the first word made.

Full circle words: art, arty, army, arm, harm, harp, harpy, happy, nappy, nap, nan, dan, dart, art

5. Reading Words Ask children to read these words: • **body, happy, mystery, sympathy**	**10. Word Dictation** Ask children to tap for the sounds and write: • **body, happy, mystery, sympathy**
6. Reading Sentences (See page 114) The model has a slim body. "I am happy," said Danny. Will you explain the mystery? The sympathy card was sad.	**11. Sentence Dictation** (See page 114) The model has a slim body. "I am happy," said Danny. Will you explain the mystery? The sympathy card was sad. After writing, children read back sounds, words and sentences.

Snappy Lesson 15

STEP 3.1

Sound /ee/ written as ie

Learning Objectives: to learn the main ways of spelling the sound /ee/; to blend and segment words and sentences containing ie

Success Criteria: to read words and sentences containing ie spelling of sound /ee/ and write dictated words and sentences with 100% accuracy

Reading	Spelling
1. Review Sounds (show as pack) • ai a-e ay ey a ee ea e e-e y	**7. Write Sounds** • ai a-e ay ey a ee ea e e-e y
2. New Spelling: ie Show the flashcard for **ie**. Then with all the phonemes play the **Grab Game**. With the cards on the table, say a sound and ask the children to 'grab' for the letter. **Fingertips Freeze** when they touch the flashcard. Only allow one 'grab'.	**8. New Spelling: ie** Model writing the letters on the board and talk through letter formation from exit stroke of first letter to start point of the next letter for joined-up writing. **Sky Write** the letters together. Ask children to write the sound on their whiteboards or paper. Check the letter formation for the correct start points, exit strokes and place on the line.
3. Oral Blending (Robot Game) Play the **Robot Game**. Pretend to be a Robot who can only speak in sounds (robot speech), moving arms back and forth like robot arms, in time with each sound. • Say the sounds **th-ie-f**, ask children to listen and say the word**.** • Repeat for: **shield, field, priest**	**9. Oral Segmenting (Phoneme Fingers)** Say a word and the children use **Phoneme Fingers** to flick their fingers for each sound in: • **b-r-ie-f, sh-r-ie-k, y-ie-l-d, ch-ie-f**

4. Manipulating (Swap) Sounds

Stick vowel cards at the top of the board: **ie**. Stick consonant cards at the bottom: **b d f l r y sh ch th**

Play the **Full Circle Word Game** using the letters on the board to make a word. Ask the children to use **Phoneme Fingers** for each sound in the word. Read the word to the children. Ask a child to change one or more sounds in the word, swapping card/s from the word with card/s at either the bottom or the top of the board. Use **Phoneme Fingers** to make and read the new word. Continue the game changing one sound at a time until you get back to the first word made.

Full circle words: field, shield, yield, field, or: **chief, brief, thief, chief**

5. Reading Words Ask children to read these words: • **thief, shield, field, priest**	**10. Word Dictation** Ask children to tap for the sounds and write: • **thief, shield, field, priest**
6. Reading Sentences (See page 114) The thief was sent to jail. Can umbrellas shield us from the sun? The sheep ate the grass in the field. The priest has a strong belief.	**11. Sentence Dictation** (See page 114) The thief was sent to jail. Can umbrellas shield us from the sun? The sheep ate the grass in the field. The priest has a strong belief. After writing, children read back sounds, words and sentences.

Snappy Lesson 16 *FastTrack*

STEP 3.1

Review: Sound /ee/ written as ee, ea, e, e-e, y, ie

Learning Objectives: to review a set of letter/sound correspondences; to learn the main ways of spelling the sound /ee/, read these spelling choices in words and sentences and write them in dictated words and sentences.

Example grid:

ee	ea	e	e-e	y	ie
see	eat	he	these	body	thief
feel	tea	me	eve	copy	brief
feet	read	she	theme	dusty	chief
need	team	we	complete	happy	field
tree	speak	be	extreme	baby	shriek
sheep	cream	frequent		very	

1. Draw a blank six-column grid on the board and explain that the group will be finding the main ways that the sound /ee/ can be written down.

2. Show the flashcard for /ee/ and ask children the main ways of writing the /ee/ sound. They may use letter names. Write the graphemes at the top of the columns on the grid.

3. Ask the children to say a word that contains the sound /ee/ and then to say which column it goes into. Write the choice in the correct column.

4. Ask the children to continue to generate examples while you write them in the correct column. There are some examples shown in the grid above if the children need prompting. Keep going until the columns are full.

5. Ask one child to come to the board, read the words in that column, underline the pattern, and comment on the position of the alternative spelling pattern in the word (i.e. beginning, middle or end).

6. Ask children to come to the board in turn until all of the alternative spelling patterns have been read, underlined and the position of the alternative spelling pattern commented on.

7. Children copy the grid into their books. Explain that they can add to this over time. Alternatively, make copies of the grid (see page 115) and stick these into the children's books. Explain that the words in this grid may not be exactly the same as those the children came up with.

8. Remove the grid from the board and dictate words (see example grid above) and the following sentences to the group for them to write down on a clean page or mini-whiteboard.

   Cats need to see in the dark.
   The pot of tea is hot.
   He will be next to me.
   These gifts are for you.
   She was a very happy baby.
   The thief ran to the field.

9. After writing the dictation, ask the children to read back a selection of words and sentences. Check for correct spelling choices and punctuation.

10. Ask the children to write a sentence of their own, using one of the words they have encountered. Listen to the children say the sentences aloud first. Moderate grammar and check for correct spelling choices and punctuation.

Snappy Lesson 17

STEP 3.1

Sound /ie/ written as ie

Learning Objectives: to learn the main ways of spelling the sound /ie/; to blend and segment words and sentences containing ie

Success Criteria: to read words and sentences containing ie spelling of sound /ie/ and write dictated words and sentences with 100% accuracy

Reading	Spelling
1. Review Sounds (show as pack) • ee ea e e-e y	**8. Write Sounds** • ee ea e e-e y
2. Spelling: ie Show the flashcard for **ie**. Then with all the phonemes play the **Grab Game**. With the cards on the table, say a sound and ask the children to 'grab' for the letter. **Fingertips Freeze** when they touch the flashcard. Only allow one 'grab'.	**9. Spelling: ie** Model writing the letters on the board and talk through letter formation from exit stroke of first letter to start point of the next letter for joined-up writing. **Sky Write** the letters together. Ask children to write the sound on their whiteboards or paper. Check the letter formation for the correct start points, exit strokes and place on the line.
3. Oral Blending (Robot Game) Play the **Robot Game**. Pretend to be a Robot who can only speak in sounds (robot speech), moving arms back and forth like robot arms, in time with each sound. • Say the sounds **p-ie**, ask children to listen and say the word**.** • Repeat for: **tie, tries, cries**	**10. Oral Segmenting (Phoneme Fingers)** Say a word and the children use **Phoneme Fingers** to flick their fingers for each sound in: • **p-ie, t-ie, t-r-ie-s, c-r-ie-s**
4. Manipulating (Swap) Sounds Stick vowel cards at the top of the board: **a i ay ie**. Stick consonant cards at the bottom: **l p s t** Play the **Full Circle Word Game** using the letters on the board to make a word. Ask the children to use **Phoneme Fingers** for each sound in the word. Read the word to the children. Ask a child to change one or more sounds in the word, swapping card/s from the word with card/s at either the bottom or the top of the board. Use **Phoneme Fingers** to make and read the new word. Continue the game changing one sound at a time until you get back to the first word made. **Full circle words: pie, tie, tip, sip, sap, say, lay, lie, pie**	
5. Reading Words Ask children to read these words: • **pie, tie, tries, cries**	**11. Word Dictation** Ask children to tap for the sounds and write: • **pie, tie, tries, cries**
6. Reading Tricky Words: great • Show flashcard with the tricky bit underlined. • Together, with the children, sound and say the word using the known letter/sound matches. • Point out that the word doesn't sound like this, identify the tricky bit, and provide tricky sound: the 'ea' sound /ai/. • Sound and say the word correctly together.	**12. Tricky Words Dictation: great** • Say the tricky word and remind children to watch out for the tricky bit. • Ask children to say the word, tap for the sounds and write each grapheme. Model with **Phoneme Fingers**, if necessary.
7. Reading Sentences (See page 115) We can bake a great pie for supper. Can you tie things up with string? He tries to cut the meat. The baby cries in the morning.	**13. Sentence Dictation** (See page 115) We can bake a great pie for supper. Can you tie things up with string? He tries to cut the meat. The baby cries in the morning. After writing, children read back sounds, words and sentences.

Snappy Lesson 18

STEP 3.1

Sound /ie/ written as i-e

Learning Objectives: to learn the main ways of spelling the sound /ie/; to blend and segment words and sentences containing i-e

Success Criteria: to read words and sentences containing i-e spelling of sound /ie/ and write dictated words and sentences with 100% accuracy

Reading	Spelling
1. Review Sounds (show as pack) • ee ea e e-e ie	**7. Write Sounds** • ee ea e e-e ie
2. New Spelling: i-e Show the flashcard for **i-e**. Then with all the phonemes play the **Grab Game**. With the cards on the table, say a sound and ask the children to 'grab' for the letter. **Fingertips Freeze** when they touch the flashcard. Only allow one 'grab'.	**8. New Spelling: i-e** Model writing the letters on the board and talk through letter formations. **Sky Write** the letters together. Ask children to write the sound on their whiteboards or paper. Check the letter formations for the correct start points, exit strokes and place on the line.
3. Oral Blending (Robot Game) Play the **Robot Game**. Pretend to be a Robot who can only speak in sounds (robot speech), moving arms back and forth like robot arms, in time with each sound. • Say the sounds **l-(i-e)-k**, ask children to listen and say the word. • Repeat for: **time, invite, outside**	**9. Oral Segmenting (Phoneme Fingers)** Say a word and the children use **Phoneme Fingers** to flick their fingers for each sound in: • l-(i-e)-k, t-(i-e)-m, i-n-v-(i-e)-t, ou-t-s-(i-e)-d

4. Manipulating (Swap) Sounds

Stick vowel cards at the top of the board: **i ay ee ie i-e**. Stick consonant cards at the bottom: **d l r s t**

Play the **Full Circle Word Game** using the letters on the board to make a word. Use two separate cards to make the split digraph i-e, ensuring children understand that this makes one sound. Ask the children to use **Phoneme Fingers** for each sound in the word. Read the word to the children. Ask a child to change one or more sounds in the word, swapping card/s from the word with card/s at either the bottom or the top of the board. Use **Phoneme Fingers** to make and read the new word. Continue the game changing one sound at a time until you get back to the first word made.

Full circle words: rid, ride, tide, tied, lied, lay, say, see, seed, side, ride, rid

5. Reading Words Ask children to read these words: • like, time, invite, outside	**10. Word Dictation** Ask children to tap for the sounds and write: • like, time, invite, outside
6. Reading Sentences (See page 115) They like to come for tea. It's time for bed. She will invite him to the party. The children play outside.	**11. Sentence Dictation** (See page 115) They like to come for tea. It's time for bed. She will invite him to the party. The children play outside. After writing, children read back sounds, words and sentences.

Snappy Lesson 19

STEP 3.1

Sound /ie/ written as igh

Learning Objectives: to learn the main ways of spelling the sound /ie/; to blend and segment words and sentences containing igh

Success Criteria: to read words and sentences containing igh spelling of sound /ie/ and write dictated words and sentences with 100% accuracy

Reading	Spelling
1. Review Sounds (show as pack) • ee ea e e-e ie i-e	**7. Write Sounds** • ee ea e e-e ie i-e
2. New Spelling: igh Show the flashcard for **igh**. Then with all the phonemes play the **Grab Game**. With the cards on the table, say a sound and ask the children to 'grab' for the letter. **Fingertips Freeze** when they touch the flashcard. Only allow one 'grab'.	**8. New Spelling: igh** Model writing the letters on the board and talk through letter formation from exit stroke of first letter to start point of the next letter for joined-up writing. **Sky Write** the letters together. Ask children to write the sound on their whiteboards or paper. Check the letter formation for the correct start points, exit strokes and place on the line.
3. Oral Blending (Robot Game) Play the **Robot Game**. Pretend to be a Robot who can only speak in sounds (robot speech), moving arms back and forth like robot arms, in time with each sound. • Say the sounds **h-igh**, ask children to listen and say the word. • Repeat for: **sigh, light, night**	**9. Oral Segmenting (Phoneme Fingers)** Say a word and the children use **Phoneme Fingers** to flick their fingers for each sound in: • **h-igh, s-igh, l-igh-t, n-igh-t**

4. Manipulating (Swap) Sounds

Stick vowel cards at the top of the board: **i a-e a igh**. Stick consonant cards at the bottom: **f m r t**

Play the **Full Circle Word Game** using the letters on the board to make a word. Use two separate cards to make the split digraph a-e, ensuring children understand that this makes one sound. Ask the children to use **Phoneme Fingers** for each sound in the word. Read the word to the children. Ask a child to change one or more sounds in the word, swapping card/s from the word with card/s at either the bottom or the top of the board. Use **Phoneme Fingers** to make and read the new word. Continue the game changing one sound at a time until you get back to the first word made.

Full circle words: fight, fit, fate, rate, right, might, mate, mat, fat, fight

5. Reading Words Ask children to read these words: • **high, sigh, light, night**	**10. Word Dictation** Ask children to tap for the sounds and write: • **high, sigh, light, night**
6. Reading Sentences (See page 116) Did Shane get a high mark? Bob gave a loud sigh. The garden light helps us to see. It is dark at night.	**11. Sentence Dictation** (See page 116) Did Shane get a high mark? Bob gave a loud sigh. The garden light helps us to see. It is dark at night. After writing, children read back sounds, words and sentences.

Snappy Lesson 20

STEP 3.1

Sound /ie/ written as y

Learning Objectives: to learn the main ways of spelling the sound /ie/; to blend and segment words and sentences containing y

Success Criteria: to read words and sentences containing y spelling of sound /ie/ and write dictated words and sentences with 100% accuracy

Reading	Spelling
1. Review Sounds (show as pack) • ee ea e e-e ie i-e igh	**7. Write Sounds** • ee ea e e-e ie i-e igh
2. New Spelling: y Show the flashcard for **y**. Then with all the phonemes play the **Grab Game**. With the cards on the table, say a sound and ask the children to 'grab' for the letter. **Fingertips Freeze** when they touch the flashcard. Only allow one 'grab'.	**8. New Spelling: y** Model writing the letter on the board and talk through letter formation. **Sky Write** the letter together. Ask children to write the sound on their whiteboards or paper. Check the letter formation for the correct start point, exit stroke and place on the line.
3. Oral Blending (Robot Game) Play the **Robot Game**. Pretend to be a Robot who can only speak in sounds (robot speech), moving arms back and forth like robot arms, in time with each sound. • Say the sounds **m-y**, ask children to listen and say the word. • Repeat for: **by, dry, sky**	**9. Oral Segmenting (Phoneme Fingers)** Say a word and the children use **Phoneme Fingers** to flick their fingers for each sound in: • **m-y, b-y, d-r-y, s-k-y**

4. Manipulating (Swap) Sounds

Stick vowel cards at the top of the board: **i a-e ie igh y**. Stick consonant cards at the bottom: **d f l r t**

Play the **Full Circle Word Game** using the letters on the board to make a word. Use two separate cards to make the split digraph a-e, ensuring children understand that this makes one sound. Ask the children to use **Phoneme Fingers** for each sound in the word. Read the word to the children. Ask a child to change one or more sounds in the word, swapping card/s from the word with card/s at either the bottom or the top of the board. Use **Phoneme Fingers** to make and read the new word. Continue the game changing one sound at a time until you get back to the first word made.

Full circle words: fry, fly, flight, light, lit, late, date, die, dry, fry

5. Reading Words Ask children to read these words: • my, by, dry, sky	**10. Word Dictation** Ask children to tap for the sounds and write: • my, by, dry, sky
6. Reading Sentences (See page 116) The train stops by the sea. There are fish in my pond. An umbrella keeps you dry. The sun shines in the sky.	**11. Sentence Dictation** (See page 116) The train stops by the sea. There are fish in my pond. An umbrella keeps you dry. The sun shines in the sky. After writing, children read back sounds, words and sentences.

STEP 3.1

Snappy Lesson 21

Sound /ie/ written as i

Learning Objectives: to learn the main ways of spelling the sound /ie/; to blend and segment words and sentences containing i

Success Criteria: to read words and sentences containing i spelling of sound /ie/ and write dictated words and sentences with 100% accuracy

Reading	Spelling
1. Review Sounds (show as pack) • ee ea e e-e ie i-e igh	**7. Write Sounds** • ee ea e e-e ie i-e igh y
2. New Spelling: i Show the flashcard for **i**. Then with all the phonemes play the **Grab Game**. With the cards on the table, say a sound and ask the children to 'grab' for the letter. **Fingertips Freeze** when they touch the flashcard. Only allow one 'grab'.	**8. New Spelling: i** Model writing the letter on the board and talk through letter formation. **Sky Write** the letter together. Ask children to write the sound on their whiteboards or paper. Check the letter formation for the correct start point, exit stroke and place on the line.
3. Oral Blending (Robot Game) Play the **Robot Game**. Pretend to be a Robot who can only speak in sounds (robot speech), moving arms back and forth like robot arms, in time with each sound. • Say the sounds **p-i-n-t**, ask children to listen and say the word. • Repeat for: **child, remind, behind**	**9. Oral Segmenting (Phoneme Fingers)** Say a word and the children use **Phoneme Fingers** to flick their fingers for each sound in: • **p-i-n-t, ch-i-l-d, r-e-m-i-n-d, b-e-h-i-n-d**

4. Manipulating (Swap) Sounds

Stick vowel cards at the top of the board: **i**. Stick consonant cards at the bottom: **d f k m n p t**

Play the **Full Circle Word Game** using the letters on the board to make a word. Ask the children to use **Phoneme Fingers** for each sound in the word. Read the word to the children. Ask a child to change one or more sounds in the word, swapping card/s from the word with card/s at either the bottom or the top of the board. Use **Phoneme Fingers** to make and read the new word. Continue the game changing one sound at a time until you get back to the first word made.

Full circle words: pin, pint, pit, kit, kid, kind, mind, find, fin, pin

5. Reading Words Ask children to read these words: • **pint, child, remind, behind**	**10. Word Dictation** Ask children to tap for the sounds and write: • **pint, child, remind, behind**
6. Reading Sentences (See page 116) **The milkman left a pint of milk.** **The child tried to float in the sea.** **You remind me of the queen.** **The moon went behind the cloud.**	**11. Sentence Dictation** (See page 116) **The milkman left a pint of milk.** **The child tried to float in the sea.** **You remind me of the queen.** **The moon went behind the cloud.** After writing, children read back sounds, words and sentences.

Snappy Lesson 22 *FastTrack*

STEP 3.1

Review: Sound /ie/ written as ie, i-e, igh, y, i

Learning Objectives: to review a set of letter/sound correspondences; to learn the main ways of spelling the sound /ie/, read these spelling choices in words and sentences and write them in dictated words and sentences.

Example grid:

ie	i-e	igh	y	i
pie	like	high	by	mind
lie	time	light	my	find
tie	ride	night	try	wild
cried	bike	fight	sky	kind
tried	shine	bright	deny	child
fried	prize	tonight	reply	blind

1. Draw a blank five-column grid on the board and explain that the group will be finding the main ways that the sound /ie/ can be written down.

2. Show the flashcard for /ie/ and ask children the main ways of writing the /ie/ sound. They may use letter names. Write the graphemes at the top of the columns on the grid.

3. Ask the children to say a word that contains the sound /ie/ and then to say which column it goes into. Write the choice in the correct column.

4. Ask the children to continue to generate examples while you write them in the correct column. There are some examples shown in the grid above if the children need prompting. Keep going until the columns are full.

5. Ask one child to come to the board, read the words in that column, underline the pattern, and comment on the position of the alternative spelling pattern in the word (i.e. beginning, middle or end).

6. Ask children to come to the board in turn until all of the alternative spelling patterns have been read, underlined and the position of the alternative spelling pattern commented on.

7. Children copy the grid into their books. Explain that they can add to this over time. Alternatively, make copies of the grid (see page 117) and stick these into the children's books. Explain that the words in this grid may not be exactly the same as those the children came up with.

8. Remove the grid from the board and dictate words (see example grid above) and the following sentences to the group for them to write down on a clean page or mini-whiteboard.

   Bob tried to tie the rope.
   I like to see the stars shine.
   The night light is too bright.
   She will try to reply to my note.
   This kind child will find the cat.

9. After writing the dictation, ask the children to read back a selection of words and sentences. Check for correct spelling choices and punctuation.

10. Ask the children to write a sentence of their own, using one of the words they have encountered. Listen to the children say the sentences aloud first. Moderate grammar and check for correct spelling choices and punctuation.

Snappy Lesson 23

STEP 3.1

Sound /oa/ written as oa

Learning Objectives: to learn the main ways of spelling the sound /oa/; to blend and segment words and sentences containing oa

Success Criteria: to read words and sentences containing oa spelling of sound /oa/ and write dictated words and sentences with 100% accuracy

Reading	Spelling
1. Review Sounds (show as pack) • ie i-e igh y i	**8. Write Sounds** • ie i-e igh y i
2. Spelling: oa Show the flashcard for **i**. Then with all the phonemes play the **Grab Game**. With the cards on the table, say a sound and ask the children to 'grab' for the letter. **Fingertips Freeze** when they touch the flashcard. Only allow one 'grab'.	**9. Spelling: oa** Model writing the letters on the board and talk through letter formation from exit stroke of first letter to start point of the next letter for joined-up writing. **Sky Write** the letters together. Ask children to write the sound on their whiteboards or paper. Check the letter formation for the correct start points, exit strokes and place on the line.
3. Oral Blending (Robot Game) Play the **Robot Game**. Pretend to be a Robot who can only speak in sounds (robot speech), moving arms back and forth like robot arms, in time with each sound. • Say the sounds **oa-k**, ask children to listen and say the word. • Repeat for: **Joan, coach, toast**	**10. Oral Segmenting (Phoneme Fingers)** Say a word and the children use **Phoneme Fingers** to flick their fingers for each sound in: • **oa-k, J-oa-n, c-oa-ch, t-oa-s-t**

4. Manipulating (Swap) Sounds

Stick vowel cards at the top of the board: **a o oa**. Stick consonant cards at the bottom: **b c s t**

Play the **Full Circle Word Game** using the letters on the board to make a word. Ask the children to use **Phoneme Fingers** for each sound in the word. Read the word to the children. Ask a child to change one or more sounds in the word, swapping card/s from the word with card/s at either the bottom or the top of the board. Use **Phoneme Fingers** to make and read the new word. Continue the game changing one sound at a time until you get back to the first word made.

Full circle words: cot, coat, cat, bat, boat, boast, coast, cost, cot

5. Reading Words Ask children to read these words: • **oak, Joan, coach, toast**	**11. Word Dictation** Ask children to tap for the sounds and write: • **oak, Joan, coach, toast**
6. Reading Tricky Words: eyes • Show flashcard with the tricky bits underlined. • Together, with the children, sound and say the word using the known letter/sound matches. • Point out that the word doesn't sound like this, identify the tricky bits, and provide tricky sounds: the 'eye' sounds /ie/ and the 's' sounds /z/. • Sound and say the word correctly together.	**12. Tricky Words Dictation: eyes** • Say the tricky word and remind children to watch out for the tricky bits. • Ask children to say the word, tap for the sounds and write each grapheme. Model with **Phoneme Fingers**, if necessary.
7. Reading Sentences (See page 117) Is this wood oak or beech? Joan went for an eye test. The coach went round the corner. He put the toast on a plate.	**13. Sentence Dictation** (See page 117) Is this wood oak or beech? Joan went for an eye test. The coach went round the corner. He put the toast on a plate. After writing, children read back sounds, words and sentences.

STEP 3.1

Snappy Lesson 24

Sound /oa/ written as o-e

Learning Objectives: to learn the main ways of spelling the sound/oa/; to blend and segment words and sentences containing o-e

Success Criteria: to read words and sentences containing o-e spelling of sound /oa/ and write dictated words and sentences with 100% accuracy

Reading	Spelling
1. Review Sounds (show as pack) • ie i-e igh y i oa	**7. Write Sounds** • ie i-e igh y i oa
2. New Spelling: o-e Show the flashcard for **o-e**. Then with all the phonemes play the **Grab Game**. With the cards on the table, say a sound and ask the children to 'grab' for the letter. **Fingertips Freeze** when they touch the flashcard. Only allow one 'grab'.	**8. New Spelling: o-e** Model writing the letters on the board and talk through letter formations. **Sky Write** the letters together. Ask children to write the sound on their whiteboards or paper. Check the letter formations for the correct start points, exit strokes and place on the line.
3. Oral Blending (Robot Game) Play the **Robot Game**. Pretend to be a Robot who can only speak in sounds (robot speech), moving arms back and forth like robot arms, in time with each sound. • Say the sounds **p-(o-e)-l**, ask children to listen and say the word. • Repeat for: **woke, note, envelope**	**9. Oral Segmenting (Phoneme Fingers)** Say a word and the children use **Phoneme Fingers** to flick their fingers for each sound in: • p-(o-e)-l, w-(o-e)-k, n-(o-e)-t, e-n-v-e-l-(o-e)-p
4. Manipulating (Swap) Sounds Stick vowel cards at the top of the board: **o o-e**. Stick consonant cards at the bottom: **c h n p r t** Play the **Full Circle Word Game** using the letters on the board to make a word. Use two separate cards to make the split digraph o-e, ensuring children understand that this makes one sound. Ask the children to use **Phoneme Fingers** for each sound in the word. Read the word to the children. Ask a child to change one or more sounds in the word, swapping card/s from the word with card/s at either the bottom or the top of the board. Use **Phoneme Fingers** to make and read the new word. Continue the game changing one sound at a time until you get back to the first word made. **Full circle words: not, note, rote, rot, hot, hop, hope, cope, cop, cot, not**	
5. Reading Words Ask children to read these words: • pole, woke, note, envelope	**10. Word Dictation** Ask children to tap for the sounds and write: • pole, woke, note, envelope
6. Reading Sentences (See page 117) Was there a flag on the pole? They woke at three in the morning. The note invited him to the party. I put the letter in an envelope.	**11. Sentence Dictation** (See page 117) Was there a flag on the pole? They woke at three in the morning. The note invited him to the party. I put the letter in an envelope. After writing, children read back sounds, words and sentences.

Look out for tricky word: put

Snappy Lesson 25

STEP 3.1

Sound /oa/ written as o

Learning Objectives: to learn the main ways of spelling the sound /oa/; to blend and segment words and sentences containing o

Success Criteria: to read words and sentences containing o spelling of sound /oa/ and write dictated words and sentences with 100% accuracy

Reading	Spelling
1. Review Sounds (show as pack) • ie i-e igh y i oa o-e	**7. Write Sounds** • ie i-e igh y i oa o-e
2. New Spelling: o Show the flashcard for **o**. Then with all the phonemes play the **Grab Game**. With the cards on the table, say a sound and ask the children to 'grab' for the letter. **Fingertips Freeze** when they touch the flashcard. Only allow one 'grab'.	**8. New Spelling: o** Model writing the letter on the board and talk through letter formation. **Sky Write** the letter together. Ask children to write the sound on their whiteboards or paper. Check the letter formation for the correct start points, exit strokes and place on the line.
3. Oral Blending (Robot Game) Play the **Robot Game**. Pretend to be a Robot who can only speak in sounds (robot speech), moving arms back and forth like robot arms, in time with each sound. • Say the sounds **g-o**, ask children to listen and say the word. • Repeat for: **gold, cold, both**	**9. Oral Segmenting (Phoneme Fingers)** Say a word and the children use **Phoneme Fingers** to flick their fingers for each sound in: • **g-o, g-o-l-d, c-o-l-d, b-o-th**
4. Manipulating (Swap) Sounds Stick vowel cards at the top of the board: **o**. Stick consonant cards at the bottom: **d g n s t ng** Play the **Full Circle Word Game** using the letters on the board to make a word. Ask the children to use **Phoneme Fingers** for each sound in the word. Read the word to the children. Ask a child to change one or more sounds in the word, swapping card/s from the word with card/s at either the bottom or the top of the board. Use **Phoneme Fingers** to make and read the new word. Continue the game changing one sound at a time until you get back to the first word made. **Full circle words: not, no, go, got, gong, song, so, sod, nod, not**	
5. Reading Words Ask children to read these words: • **go, gold, cold, both**	**10. Word Dictation** Ask children to tap for the sounds and write: • **go, gold, cold, both**
6. Reading Sentences (See page 118) Please go away. He kept gold bars in his safe. Are you cold? Both sisters were ill.	**11. Sentence Dictation** (See page 118) Please go away. He kept gold bars in his safe. Are you cold? Both sisters were ill. After writing, children read back sounds, words and sentences.

Look out for tricky word: please

Snappy Lesson 26

STEP 3.1

Sound /oa/ written as ow

Learning Objectives: to learn the main ways of spelling the sound /oa/; to blend and segment words and sentences containing ow

Success Criteria: to read words and sentences containing ow spelling of sound /oa/ and write dictated words and sentences with 100% accuracy

Reading	Spelling
1. Review Sounds (show as pack) • ie i-e igh y i oa o-e o	**7. Write Sounds** • ie i-e igh y i oa o-e o
2. New Spelling: OW Show the flashcard for **ow**. Then with all the phonemes play the **Grab Game**. With the cards on the table, say a sound and ask the children to 'grab' for the letter. **Fingertips Freeze** when they touch the flashcard. Only allow one 'grab'.	**8. New Spelling: OW** Model writing the letters on the board and talk through letter formation from exit stroke of first letter to start point of the next letter for joined-up writing. **Sky Write** the letters together. Ask children to write the sound on their whiteboards or paper. Check the letter formation for the correct start points, exit strokes and place on the line.
3. Oral Blending (Robot Game) Play the **Robot Game**. Pretend to be a Robot who can only speak in sounds (robot speech), moving arms back and forth like robot arms, in time with each sound. • Say the sounds **g-l-ow**, ask children to listen and say the word. • Repeat for: **blow, snow, show**	**9. Oral Segmenting (Phoneme Fingers)** Say a word and the children use **Phoneme Fingers** to flick their fingers for each sound in: • g-l-ow, b-l-ow, s-n-ow, sh-ow

4. Manipulating (Swap) Sounds

Stick vowel cards at the top of the board: **o oa ow**
Stick consonant cards at the bottom: **b f g l t**

Play the **Full Circle Word Game** using the letters on the board to make a word. Ask the children to use **Phoneme Fingers** for each sound in the word. Read the word to the children. Ask a child to change one or more sounds in the word, swapping card/s from the word with card/s at either the bottom or the top of the board. Use **Phoneme Fingers** to make and read the new word. Continue the game changing one sound at a time until you get back to the first word made.

Full circle words: low, glow, flow, float, bloat, blot, lot, low

5. Reading Words Ask children to read these words: • **glow, blow, snow, show**	**10. Word Dictation** Ask children to tap for the sounds and write: • **glow, blow, snow, show**
6. Reading Sentences (See page 118) **The torch glows with a bright light.** **Will the wind blow out the flame?** **The snow lies on the ground.** **Show me your bike.**	**11. Sentence Dictation** (See page 118) **The torch glows with a bright light.** **Will the wind blow out the flame?** **The snow lies on the ground.** **Show me your bike.** After writing, children read back sounds, words and sentences.

Snappy Lesson 27

STEP 3.1

Sound /oa/ written as ou

Learning Objectives: to learn the main ways of spelling the sound /oa/; to blend and segment words and sentences containing ou

Success Criteria: to read words and sentences containing ou spelling of sound /oa/ and write dictated words and a sentences with 100% accuracy

Reading	Spelling
1. Review Sounds (show as pack) • ie i-e igh y i oa o-e o ow	**7. Write Sounds** • ie i-e igh y i oa o-e o ow
2. New Spelling: ou Show the flashcard for **ou**. Then with all the phonemes play the **Grab Game**. With the cards on the table, say a sound and ask the children to 'grab' for the letter. **Fingertips Freeze** when they touch the flashcard. Only allow one 'grab'.	**8. New Spelling: ou** Model writing the letters on the board and talk through letter formation from exit stroke of first letter to start point of the next letter for joined-up writing. **Sky Write** the letters together. Ask children to write the sound on their whiteboards or paper. Check the letter formation for the correct start points, exit strokes and place on the line.
3. Oral Blending (Robot Game) Play the **Robot Game**. Pretend to be a Robot who can only speak in sounds (robot speech), moving arms back and forth like robot arms, in time with each sound. • Say the sounds s-ou-l, ask children to listen and say the word. • Repeat for: **soul, mould, poultry, smoulder**	**9. Oral Segmenting (Phoneme Fingers)** Say a word and the children use **Phoneme Fingers** to flick their fingers for each sound in: **s-ou-l, m-ou-l-d-y, b-ou-l-d-er, sh-ou-l-d-er**

4. Manipulating (Swap) Sounds

Stick vowel cards at the top of the board: **er y ou**
Stick consonant cards at the bottom: **d l m s sh**

Play the **Full Circle Word Game** using the letters on the board to make a word. Ask the children to use **Phoneme Fingers** for each sound in the word. Read the word to the children. Ask a child to change one or more sounds in the word, swapping card/s from the word with card/s at either the bottom or the top of the board. Use **Phoneme Fingers** to make and read the new word. Continue the game changing one sound at a time until you get back to the first word made.

Full circle words: soul, mould, mouldy, shoulder, smoulder, mould, soul

5. Reading Words Ask children to read these words: • soul, mould, poultry, smoulder	**10. Word Dictation** Ask children to tap for the sounds and write: • soul, mouldy, boulder, shoulder
6. Reading Sentences (See page 118) I can smell mould in the damp room. Charlie was the life and soul of the party. The farmer kept poultry in the back yard. The ashes began to smoulder.	**11. Sentence Dictation** (See page 118) I can smell mould in the damp room. Charlie was the life and soul of the party. The farmer kept poultry in the back yard. The ashes began to smoulder. After writing, children read back sounds, words and sentences.

Snappy Lesson 28 — FastTrack

STEP 3.1

Review: Sound /oa/ written as oa, o-e, o, ow, ou

Learning Objectives: to review a set of letter/sound correspondences; to learn the main ways of spelling the sound /oa/, read these spelling choices in words and sentences and write them in dictated words and sentences.

Example grid:

oa	o-e	o	ow	ou
coat	home	no	low	soul
goat	hope	so	grow	mouldy
road	nose	go	snow	shoulder
foal	those	old	slow	boulder
boast	spoke	don't	window	
float	stone	most	yellow	

1. Draw a blank five-column grid on the board and explain that the group will be finding the main ways that the sound /oa/ can be written down.

2. Show the flashcard for /oa/ and ask children the main ways of writing the /oa/ sound. They may use letter names. Write the graphemes at the top of the columns on the grid.

3. Ask the children to say a word that contains the sound /oa/ and then to say which column it goes into. Write the choice in the correct column.

4. Ask the children to continue to generate examples while you write them in the correct column. There are some examples shown in the grid above if the children need prompting. Keep going until the columns are full.

5. Ask one child to come to the board, read the words in that column, underline the pattern, and comment on the position of the alternative spelling pattern in the word (i.e. beginning, middle or end).

6. Ask children to come to the board in turn until all of the alternative spelling patterns have been read, underlined and the position of the alternative spelling pattern commented on.

7. Children copy the grid into their books. Explain that they can add to this over time. Alternatively, make copies of the grid (see page 119) and stick these into the children's books. Explain that the words in this grid may not be exactly the same as those the children came up with.

8. Remove the grid from the board and dictate words (see example grid above) and the following sentences to the group for them to write down on a clean page or mini-whiteboard.

   The goat was next to the road.
   Those stones look like bones.
   As it is so cold, we will not go.
   The yellow train is slow in the snow.
   Don't eat the mouldy cake.

9. After writing the dictation, ask the children to read back a selection of words and sentences. Check for correct spelling choices and punctuation.

10. Ask the children to write a sentence of their own, using one of the words they have encountered. Listen to the children say the sentences aloud first. Moderate grammar and check for correct spelling choices and punctuation.

Snappy Lesson 29

STEP 3.1

Sound /ue/ written as ue

Learning Objectives: to learn the main ways of spelling the sound /ue/; to blend and segment words and sentences containing ue

Success Criteria: to read words and sentences containing ue spelling of sound /ue/ and write dictated words and sentences with 100% accuracy

Reading	Spelling
1. Review Sounds (show as pack) • oa o-e o ow	**8. Write Sounds** • oa o-e o ow
2. Spelling: ue Show the flashcard for **ue**. Then with all the phonemes play the **Grab Game**. With the cards on the table, say a sound and ask the children to 'grab' for the letter. **Fingertips Freeze** when they touch the flashcard. Only allow one 'grab'.	**9. Spelling: ue** Model writing the letters on the board and talk through letter formation from exit stroke of first letter to start point of the next letter for joined-up writing. **Sky Write** the letters together. Ask children to write the sound on their whiteboards or paper. Check the letter formation for the correct start points, exit strokes and place on the line.
3. Oral Blending (Robot Game) Play the **Robot Game**. Pretend to be a Robot who can only speak in sounds (robot speech), moving arms back and forth like robot arms, in time with each sound. • Say the sounds **v-e-n-ue**, ask children to listen and say the **word**. • Repeat for: **value, statue, rescue**	**10. Oral Segmenting (Phoneme Fingers)** Say a word and the children use **Phoneme Fingers** to flick their fingers for each sound in: • v-e-n-ue, v-a-l-ue, s-t-a-t-ue, r-e-s-c-ue
4. Manipulating (Swap) Sounds Stick vowel cards at the top of the board: **ay ue**. Stick consonant cards at the bottom: **c d h l** Play the **Full Circle Word Game** using the letters on the board to make a word. Ask the children to use **Phoneme Fingers** for each sound in the word. Read the word to the children. Ask a child to change one or more sounds in the word, swapping card/s from the word with card/s at either the bottom or the top of the board. Use **Phoneme Fingers** to make and read the new word. Continue the game changing one sound at a time until you get back to the first word made. **Full circle words: due, day, lay, hay, hue, cue, due**	
5. Reading Words Ask children to read these words: • venue, value, statue, rescue	**11. Word Dictation** Ask children to tap for the sounds and write: • venue, value, statue, rescue
6. Reading Tricky Words: when • Show flashcard with the tricky bit underlined. • Together, with the children, sound and say the word using the known letter/sound matches. • Point out that the word doesn't sound like this, identify the tricky bit, and provide tricky sound: the 'wh' sounds /w/. • Sound and say the word correctly together.	**12. Tricky Words Dictation: when** • Say the tricky word and remind children to watch out for the tricky bit. • Ask children to say the word, tap for the sounds and write each grapheme. Model with **Phoneme Fingers**, if necessary.
7. Reading Sentences (See page 119) The bar was the venue for the quiz. Were the bananas good value? When was the statue painted? The rescue party found the child.	**13. Sentence Dictation** (See page 119) The bar was the venue for the quiz. Were the bananas good value? When was the statue painted? The rescue party found the child. After writing, children read back sounds, words and sentences.

Snappy Lesson 30

STEP 3.1

Sound /ue/ written as u-e

Learning Objectives: to learn the main ways of spelling the sound/ue/; to blend and segment words and sentences containing u-e

Success Criteria: to read words and sentences containing u-e spelling of sound /ue/ and write dictated words and sentences with 100% accuracy

Reading	Spelling
1. Review Sounds (show as pack) • oa o-e o ow ue	**7. Write Sounds** • oa o-e o ow ue
2. New Spelling: u-e Show the flashcard for **u-e**. Then with all the phonemes play the **Grab Game**. With the cards on the table, say a sound and ask the children to 'grab' for the letter. **Fingertips Freeze** when they touch the flashcard. Only allow one 'grab'.	**8. New Spelling: u-e** Model writing the letters on the board and talk through letter formations. **Sky Write** the letters together. Ask children to write the sound on their whiteboards or paper. Check the letter formations for the correct start points, exit strokes and place on the line.
3. Oral Blending (Robot Game) Play the **Robot Game**. Pretend to be a Robot who can only speak in sounds (robot speech), moving arms back and forth like robot arms, in time with each sound. • Say the sounds **f-(u-e)-s**, ask children to listen and say the word. • Repeat for: **cube, tube, mule**	**9. Oral Segmenting (Phoneme Fingers)** Say a word and the children use **Phoneme Fingers** to flick their fingers for each sound in: • f-(u-e)-s, c-(u-e)-b, t-(u-e)-b, m-(u-e)-l

4. Manipulating (Swap) Sounds

Stick vowel cards at the top of the board: **u ue u-e**. Stick consonant cards at the bottom: **b c f n s t**

Play the **Full Circle Word Game** using the letters on the board to make a word. Use two separate cards to make the split digraph u-e, ensuring children understand that this makes one sound. Ask the children to use **Phoneme Fingers** for each sound in the word. Read the word to the children. Ask a child to change one or more sounds in the word, swapping card/s from the word with card/s at either the bottom or the top of the board. Use **Phoneme Fingers** to make and read the new word. Continue the game changing one sound at a time until you get back to the first word made.

Full circle words: us, use, fuse, fun, tune, tube, cube, cue, cues, us

5. Reading Words Ask children to read these words: • fuse, cube, tube, mule	**10. Word Dictation** Ask children to tap for the sounds and write: • fuse, cube, tube, mule
6. Reading Sentences (See page 119) Is there a fuse in the plug? Six of the shapes were cubes. The tube of toothpaste was empty. The farmer rode a mule to market.	**11. Sentence Dictation** (See page 119) Is there a fuse in the plug? Six of the shapes were cubes. The tube of toothpaste was empty. The farmer rode a mule to market. After writing, children read back sounds, words and sentences.

Snappy Lesson 31

STEP 3.1

Sound /ue/ written as u

Learning Objectives: to learn the main ways of spelling the sound /ue/; to blend and segment words and sentences containing u

Success Criteria: to read words and sentences containing u spelling of sound /ue/ and write dictated words and sentences with 100% accuracy

Reading	Spelling
1. Review Sounds (show as pack) • oa o-e o ow ue u-e	**7. Write Sounds** • oa o-e o ow ue u-e
2. New Spelling: u Show the flashcard for **u**. Then with all the phonemes play the **Grab Game**. With the cards on the table, say a sound and ask the children to 'grab' for the letter. **Fingertips Freeze** when they touch the flashcard. Only allow one 'grab'.	**8. New Spelling: u** Model writing the letter on the board and talk through letter formation. **Sky Write** the letter together. Ask children to write the sound on their whiteboards or paper. Check the letter formation for the correct start point, exit stroke and place on the line.
3. Oral Blending (Robot Game) Play the **Robot Game**. Pretend to be a Robot who can only speak in sounds (robot speech), moving arms back and forth like robot arms, in time with each sound. • Say the sounds **t-u-b-a**, ask children to listen and say the word. • Repeat for: **duty, unicorn, uniform**	**9. Oral Segmenting (Phoneme Fingers)** Say a word and the children use **Phoneme Fingers** to flick their fingers for each sound in: • **t-u-b-a, d-u-t-y, u-n-i-c-or-n, u-n-i-f-or-m**

4. Manipulating (Swap) Sounds

Stick vowel cards at the top of the board: **a u u-e**. Stick consonant cards at the bottom: **b h m n t**

Play the **Full Circle Word Game** using the letters on the board to make a word. Use two separate cards to make the split digraph u-e, ensuring children understand that this makes one sound. Ask the children to use **Phoneme Fingers** for each sound in the word. Read the word to the children. Ask a child to change one or more sounds in the word, swapping card/s from the word with card/s at either the bottom or the top of the board. Use **Phoneme Fingers** to make and read the new word. Continue the game changing one sound at a time until you get back to the first word made.

Full circle words: man, human, hum, hub, tub, tube, tune, tuna, tuba, tub, tab, tan, man

5. Reading Words Ask children to read these words: • **tuba, duty, unicorn, uniform**	**10. Word Dictation** Ask children to tap for the sounds and write: • **tuba, duty, unicorn, uniform**
6. Reading Sentences (See page 120) She plays the tuba. The teacher was on duty. Is a unicorn a real animal? His uniform is too big.	**11. Sentence Dictation** (See page 120) She plays the tuba. The teacher was on duty. Is a unicorn a real animal? His uniform is too big. After writing, children read back sounds, words and sentences.

Snappy Lesson 32

STEP 3.1

Sound /ue/ written as ew

Learning Objectives: learn the main ways of spelling the sound /ue/; to blend and segment words and sentences containing ew

Success Criteria: to read words and sentences containing ew spelling of sound /ue/ and write dictated words and sentences with 100% accuracy

Reading	Spelling
1. Review Sounds (show as pack) • oa o-e o ow ue u-e u	**7. Write Sounds** • oa o-e o ow ue u-e u
2. New Spelling: ew Show the flashcard for **ew**. Then with all the phonemes play the **Grab Game**. With the cards on the table, say a sound and ask the children to 'grab' for the letter. **Fingertips Freeze** when they touch the flashcard. Only allow one 'grab'.	**8. New Spelling: ew** Model writing the letters on the board and talk through letter formation from exit stroke of first letter to start point of the next letter for joined-up writing. **Sky Write** the letters together. Ask children to write the sound on their whiteboards or paper. Check the letter formation for the correct start points, exit strokes and place on the line.
3. Oral Blending (Robot Game) Play the **Robot Game**. Pretend to be a Robot who can only speak in sounds (robot speech), moving arms back and forth like robot arms, in time with each sound. • Say the sounds **d-ew**, ask children to listen and say the word. • Repeat for: **pew, stew, renew**	**9. Oral Segmenting (Phoneme Fingers)** Say a word and the children use **Phoneme Fingers** to flick their fingers for each sound in: • **d-ew, p-ew, s-t-ew, r-e-n-ew**

4. Manipulating (Swap) Sounds

Stick vowel cards at the top of the board: **ue ew**. Stick consonant cards at the bottom: **c d f n p t**

Play the **Full Circle Word Game** using the letters on the board to make a word. Ask the children to use **Phoneme Fingers** for each sound in the word. Read the word to the children. Ask a child to change one or more sounds in the word, swapping card/s from the word with card/s at either the bottom or the top of the board. Use **Phoneme Fingers** to make and read the new word. Continue the game changing one sound at a time until you get back to the first word made.

Full circle words: newt, new, dew, due, cue, pew, few, new, newt

5. Reading Words Ask children to read these words: • **dew, pew, stew, renew**	**10. Word Dictation** Ask children to tap for the sounds and write: • **dew, pew, stew, renew**
6. Reading Sentences (See page 120) **The grass was wet with dew.** **We sat in the chapel pew.** **The cook made a rabbit stew.** **I need to renew my book.**	**11. Sentence Dictation** (See page 120) **The grass was wet with dew.** **We sat in the chapel pew.** **The cook made a rabbit stew.** **I need to renew my book.** After writing, children read back sounds, words and sentences.

Snappy Lesson 33 *FastTrack*

STEP 3.1

Review: Sound /ue/ written as ue, u-e, u, ew

Learning Objectives: to review a set of letter/sound correspondences; to learn the main ways of spelling the sound /ue/, read these spelling choices in words and sentences and write them in dictated words and sentences.

Example grid:

ue	u-e	u	ew
cue	use	pupil	few
due	cube	tuna	new
argue	tune	tulip	stew
rescue	tube	music	knew
statue	confuse	human	mildew
continue	computer	stupid	

1. Draw a blank four-column grid on the board and explain that the group will be finding the main ways that the sound /ue/ can be written down.

2. Show the flashcard for /ue/ and ask children the main ways of writing the /ue/ sound. They may use letter names. Write the graphemes at the top of the columns on the grid.

3. Ask the children to say a word that contains the sound /ue/ and then to say which column it goes into. Write the choice in the correct column.

4. Ask the children to continue to generate examples while you write them in the correct column. There are some examples shown in the grid above if the children need prompting. Keep going until the columns are full.

5. Ask one child to come to the board, read the words in that column, underline the pattern, snad comment on the position of the alternative spelling pattern in the word (i.e. beginning, middle or end).

6. Ask children to come to the board in turn until all of the alternative spelling patterns have been read, underlined and the position of the alternative spelling pattern commented on.

7. Children copy the grid into their books. Explain that they can add to this over time. Alternatively, make copies of the grid (see page 120) and stick these into the children's books. Explain that the words in this grid may not be exactly the same as those the children came up with.

8. Remove the grid from the board and dictate words (see example grid above) and the following sentences to the group for them to write down on a clean page or mini-whiteboard.

    They tried to rescue the statue from the lake.
    I get confused if I use my computer.
    The pupils like playing pop music.
    A few of us knew it was stew for dinner.

9. After writing the dictation, ask the children to read back a selection of words and sentences. Check for correct spelling choices and punctuation.

10. Ask the children to write a sentence of their own, using one of the words they have encountered. Listen to the children say the sentences aloud first. Moderate grammar and check for correct spelling choices and punctuation.

Snappy Lesson 34

STEP 3.1

Sound /ar/ written as ar

Learning Objectives: to learn the main ways of spelling the sound /ar/; to blend and segment words and sentences containing ar

Success Criteria: to read words and sentences containing ar spelling of sound /ar/ and write dictated words and sentences with 100% accuracy

Reading	Spelling
1. Review Sounds (show as pack) • ue u-e u ew	**8. Write Sounds** • ue u-e u ew
2. Spelling: ar Show the flashcard for **ar**. Then with all the phonemes play the **Grab Game**. With the cards on the table, say a sound and ask the children to 'grab' for the letter. **Fingertips Freeze** when they touch the flashcard. Only allow one 'grab'.	**9. Spelling: ar** Model writing the letters on the board and talk through letter formation from exit stroke of first letter to start point of the next letter for joined-up writing. **Sky Write** the letters together. Ask children to write the sound on their whiteboards or paper. Check the letter formation for the correct start points, exit strokes and place on the line.
3. Oral Blending (Robot Game) Play the **Robot Game**. Pretend to be a Robot who can only speak in sounds (robot speech), moving arms back and forth like robot arms, in time with each sound. • Say the sounds **j-ar**, ask children to listen and say the word. • Repeat for: **far, arch, carpet**	**10. Oral Segmenting (Phoneme Fingers)** Say a word and the children use **Phoneme Fingers** to flick their fingers for each sound in: • j-ar, f-ar, ar-ch, c-ar-p-e-t
4. Manipulating (Swap) Sounds Stick vowel cards at the top of the board: **ea ar**. Stick consonant cards at the bottom: **c d h m t ch** Play the **Full Circle Word Game** using the letters on the board to make a word. Ask the children to use **Phoneme Fingers** for each sound in the word. Read the word to the children. Ask a child to change one or more sounds in the word, swapping card/s from the word with card/s at either the bottom or the top of the board. Use **Phoneme Fingers** to make and read the new word. Continue the game changing one sound at a time until you get back to the first word made. **Full circle words: car, cart, art, eat, meat, mart, chart, charm, harm, hard, card, car**	
5. Reading Words Ask children to read these words: • jar, far, arch, carpet	**11. Word Dictation** Ask children to tap for the sounds and write: • jar, far, arch, carpet
6. Reading Tricky Words: where • Show flashcard with the tricky bits underlined. • Together, with the children, sound and say the word using the known letter/sound matches. • Point out that the word doesn't sound like this, identify the tricky bits, and provide tricky sounds: the 'wh' sounds /w/ and the 'ere' sounds /air/. • Sound and say the word correctly together.	**12. Tricky Words Dictation: where** • Say the tricky word and remind children to watch out for the tricky bits. • Ask children to say the word, tap for the sounds and write each grapheme. Model with **Phoneme Fingers**, if necessary.
7. Reading Sentences (See page 121) The jar stood on the shelf. Is the sun far away? The bus went under the arch. Where is the carpet?	**13. Sentence Dictation** (See page 121) The jar stood on the shelf. Is the sun far away? The bus went under the arch. Where is the carpet? After writing, children read back sounds, words and sentences.

Snappy Lesson 35

STEP 3.1

Sound /ar/ written as a

Learning Objectives: to learn the main ways of spelling the sound /ar/; to blend and segment words and sentences containing a

Success Criteria: to read words and sentences containing a spelling of sound /ar/ and write dictated words and sentences with 100% accuracy

General Note: This is the pronounciation for the south of England but some other accents pronounce this letter a as the /a/ sound in 'cat'.

Reading	Spelling
1. Review Sounds (show as pack) • ue u-e u ew ar	**7. Write Sounds** • ue u-e u ew ar
2. New Spelling: a Show the flashcard for **a**. Then with all the phonemes play the **Grab Game**. With the cards on the table, say a sound and ask the children to 'grab' for the letter. **Fingertips Freeze** when they touch the flashcard. Only allow one 'grab'.	**8. New Spelling: a** Model writing the letter on the board and talk through letter formation. **Sky Write** the letter together. Ask children to write the sound on their whiteboards or paper. Check the letter formation for the correct start point, exit stroke and place on the line.
3. Oral Blending (Robot Game) Play the **Robot Game**. Pretend to be a Robot who can only speak in sounds (robot speech), moving arms back and forth like robot arms, in time with each sound. • Say the sounds **l-a-s-t**, ask children to listen and say the word. • Repeat for: **rather, father, lather**	**9. Oral Segmenting (Phoneme Fingers)** Say a word and the children use **Phoneme Fingers** to flick their fingers for each sound in: • l-a-s-t, r-a-th-er, f-a-th-er, l-a-th-er

4. Manipulating (Swap) Sounds

Stick vowel cards at the top of the board: **e o ar a**. Stick consonant cards at the bottom: **b p s t ss th**

Play the **Full Circle Word Game** using the letters on the board to make a word. Ask the children to use **Phoneme Fingers** for each sound in the word. Read the word to the children. Ask a child to change one or more sounds in the word, swapping card/s from the word with card/s at either the bottom or the top of the board. Use **Phoneme Fingers** to make and read the new word. Continue the game changing one sound at a time until you get back to the first word made.

Full circle words: past, part, pass, path, bath, both, Beth, bet, best, pest, past

5. Reading Words Ask children to read these words: • last, rather, father, lather	**10. Word Dictation** Ask children to tap for the sounds and write: • last, rather, father, lather
6. Reading Sentences (See page 121) At last the lights came on. The pie was rather tasty. Father likes sweet things. This soap makes a good lather.	**11. Sentence Dictation** (See page 121) At last the lights came on. The pie was rather tasty. Father likes sweet things. This soap makes a good lather. After writing, children read back sounds, words and sentences.

Snappy Lesson 36 *FastTrack*

STEP 3.1

Review: Sound /ar/ written as ar, a

Learning Objectives: to review a set of letter/sound correspondences; to learn the main ways of spelling the sound /ar/, read these spelling choices in words and sentences and write them in dictated words and sentences.

Example grid:

ar	a
bar	Father
car	rather
arm	fast
park	bath
card	last
start	grass
	class

1. Draw a blank two-column grid on the board and explain that the group will be finding the main ways that the sound /ar/ can be written down.

2. Show the flashcard for /ar/ and ask children the main ways of writing the /ar/ sound. They may use letter names. Write the graphemes at the top of the columns on the grid.

3. Ask the children to say a word that contains the sound /ar/ and then to say which column it goes into. Write the choice in the correct column.

4. Ask the children to continue to generate examples while you write them in the correct column. There are some examples shown in the grid above if the children need prompting. Keep going until the columns are full.

5. Ask one child to come to the board, read the words in that column, underline the pattern, and comment on the position of the alternative spelling pattern in the word (i.e. beginning, middle or end).

6. Ask children to come to the board in turn until all of the alternative spelling patterns have been read, underlined and the position of the alternative spelling pattern commented on.

7. Children copy the grid into their books. Explain that they can add to this over time. Alternatively, make copies of the grid (see page 121) and stick these into the children's books. Explain that the words in this grid may not be exactly the same as those the children came up with.

8. Remove the grid from the board and dictate words (see example grid above) and the following sentences to the group for them to write down on a clean page or mini-whiteboard.

    It was hard to park the car at the market.
    Her father was rather clever.

9. After writing the dictation, ask the children to read back a selection of words and sentences. Check for correct spelling choices and punctuation.

10. Ask the children to write a sentence of their own, using one of the words they have encountered. Listen to the children say the sentences aloud first. Moderate grammar and check for correct spelling choices and punctuation.

Snappy Lesson 37

STEP 3.1

Sound /er/ written as er

Learning Objectives: to learn the main ways of spelling the sound /er/; to blend and segment words and sentences containing er

Success Criteria: to read words and sentences containing er spelling of sound /er/ and write dictated words and sentences with 100% accuracy

Reading	Spelling
1. Review Sounds (show as pack) • ar a	**8. Write Sounds** • ar a
2. Spelling: er Show the flashcard for **er**. Then with all the phonemes play the **Grab Game**. With the cards on the table, say a sound and ask the children to 'grab' for the letter. **Fingertips Freeze** when they touch the flashcard. Only allow one 'grab'.	**9. Spelling: er** Model writing the letters on the board and talk through letter formation from exit stroke of first letter to start point of the next letter for joined-up writing. **Sky Write** the letters together. Ask children to write the sound on their whiteboards or paper. Check the letter formation for the correct start points, exit strokes and place on the line.
3. Oral Blending (Robot Game) Play the **Robot Game**. Pretend to be a Robot who can only speak in sounds (robot speech), moving arms back and forth like robot arms, in time with each sound. • Say the sounds **s-er-v-a-n-t**, ask children to listen and say the word. • Repeat for: **dinner, hammer, summer**	**10. Oral Segmenting (Phoneme Fingers)** Say a word and the children use **Phoneme Fingers** to flick their fingers for each sound in: • **s-er-v-a-n-t, d-i-n/n-er, h-a-m/m-er, s-u-m/m-er**
4. Manipulating (Swap) Sounds Stick vowel cards at the top of the board: **ea er** Stick consonant cards at the bottom: **b d h m p t ch** Play the **Full Circle Word Game** using the letters on the board to make a word. Ask the children to use **Phoneme Fingers** for each sound in the word. Read the word to the children. Ask a child to change one or more sounds in the word, swapping card/s from the word with card/s at either the bottom or the top of the board. Use **Phoneme Fingers** to make and read the new word. Continue the game changing one sound at a time until you get back to the first word made. **Full circle words: her, herd, herb, perm, term, team, teach, peach, pea, perm, her**	
5. Reading Words Ask children to read these words: • **servant, dinner, hammer, summer**	**11. Word Dictation** Ask children to tap for the sounds and write: • **servant, dinner, hammer, summer**
6. Reading Tricky Words: though • Show flashcard with the tricky bit underlined. • Together, with the children, sound and say the word using the known letter/sound matches. • Point out that the word doesn't sound like this, identify the tricky bit, and provide tricky sound: the 'ough' sounds /oa/. • Sound and say the word correctly together.	**12. Tricky Words Dictation: though** • Say the tricky word and remind children to watch out for the tricky bit. • Ask children to say the word, tap for the sounds and write each grapheme. Model with **Phoneme Fingers**, if necessary.
7. Reading Sentences (See page 122) The queen has lots of servants. They were late for dinner. He hit the nail with his hammer. Though we go away in the Summer, we like to have a winter holiday.	**13. Sentence Dictation** (See page 122) The queen has lots of servants. They were late for dinner. He hit the nail with his hammer. Though we go away in the Summer, we like to have a winter holiday. After writing, children read back sounds, words and sentences.

Snappy Lesson 38

STEP 3.1

Sound /er/ written as ur

Learning Objectives: to learn the main ways of spelling the sound /er/; to blend and segment words and sentences containing ur

Success Criteria: to read words and sentences containing ur spelling of sound /er/ and write dictated words and sentences with 100% accuracy

Reading	Spelling
1. Review Sounds (show as pack) • ar a er	**7. Write Sounds** • ar a er
2. New Spelling: ur Show the flashcard for **ur**. Then with all the phonemes play the **Grab Game**. With the cards on the table, say a sound and ask the children to 'grab' for the letter. **Fingertips Freeze** when they touch the flashcard. Only allow one 'grab'.	**8. New Spelling: ur** Model writing the letters on the board and talk through letter formation from exit stroke of first letter to start point of the next letter for joined-up writing. **Sky Write** the letters together. Ask children to write the sound on their whiteboards or paper. Check the letter formation for the correct start points, exit strokes and place on the line.
3. Oral Blending (Robot Game) Play the **Robot Game**. Pretend to be a Robot who can only speak in sounds (robot speech), moving arms back and forth like robot arms, in time with each sound. • Say the sounds **h-ur-t**, ask children to listen and say the word. • Repeat for: **burp, curly, Thursday**	**9. Oral Segmenting (Phoneme Fingers)** Say a word and the children use **Phoneme Fingers** to flick their fingers for each sound in: • **h-ur-t, b-ur-p, c-ur-l-y, Th-ur-s-d-ay**

4. Manipulating (Swap) Sounds

Stick vowel cards at the top of the board: **ar er ur**. Stick consonant cards at the bottom: **b c f h l n t**

Play the **Full Circle Word Game** using the letters on the board to make a word. Ask the children to use **Phoneme Fingers** for each sound in the word. Read the word to the children. Ask a child to change one or more sounds in the word, swapping card/s from the word with card/s at either the bottom or the top of the board. Use **Phoneme Fingers** to make and read the new word. Continue the game changing one sound at a time until you get back to the first word made.

Full circle words: urn, turn, burn, bert, hurt, curt, cart, carl, curl, furl, fur, urn

5. Reading Words Ask children to read these words: • **hurt, burp, curly, Thursday**	**10. Word Dictation** Ask children to tap for the sounds and write: • **hurt, burp, curly, Thursday**
6. Reading Sentences (See page 122) The sheep hurt its foot. Can a snake burp? The pig has a curly tail. Do you like Thursdays?	**11. Sentence Dictation** (See page 122) The sheep hurt its foot. Can a snake burp? The pig has a curly tail. Do you like Thursdays? After writing, children read back sounds, words and sentences.

Snappy Lesson 39

STEP 3.1

Sound /er/ written as ir

Learning Objectives: to learn the main ways of spelling the sound /er/; to blend and segment words and sentences containing ir

Success Criteria: to read words and sentences containing ir spelling of sound /er/ and write dictated words and sentences with 100% accuracy

Reading	Spelling
1. Review Sounds (show as pack) • ar a er ur	**7. Write Sounds** • ar a er ur
2. New Spelling: ir Show the flashcard for **ir**. Then with all the phonemes play the **Grab Game**. With the cards on the table, say a sound and ask the children to 'grab' for the letter. **Fingertips Freeze** when they touch the flashcard. Only allow one 'grab'.	**8. New Spelling: ir** Model writing the letters on the board and talk through letter formation from exit stroke of first letter to start point of the next letter for joined-up writing. **Sky Write** the letters together. Ask children to write the sound on their whiteboards or paper. Check the letter formation for the correct start points, exit strokes and place on the line.
3. Oral Blending (Robot Game) Play the **Robot Game**. Pretend to be a Robot who can only speak in sounds (robot speech), moving arms back and forth like robot arms, in time with each sound. • Say the sounds **b-ir-th**, ask children to listen and say the word. • Repeat for: **skirt, thirsty, thirteen**	**9. Oral Segmenting (Phoneme Fingers)** Say a word and the children use **Phoneme Fingers** to flick their fingers for each sound in: • **b-ir-th, s-k-ir-t, th-ir-s-t-y, th-ir-t-ee-n**
4. Manipulating (Swap) Sounds Stick vowel cards at the top of the board: **ir ar ur**. Stick consonant cards at the bottom: **b d f s t th** Play the **Full Circle Word Game** using the letters on the board to make a word. Ask the children to use **Phoneme Fingers** for each sound in the word. Read the word to the children. Ask a child to change one or more sounds in the word, swapping card/s from the word with card/s at either the bottom or the top of the board. Use **Phoneme Fingers** to make and read the new word. Continue the game changing one sound at a time until you get back to the first word made. **Full circle words: sir, fur, first, fir, far, bar, bard, bird, third, thirst, burst, fur, fir, sir**	
5. Reading Words Ask children to read these words: • **birth, skirt, thirsty, thirteen**	**10. Word Dictation** Ask children to tap for the sounds and write: • **birth, skirt, thirsty, thirteen**
6. Reading Sentences (See page 122) **Can a goat give birth to piglets?** **The skirt was too long.** **Jogging makes me thirsty.** **Is thirteen a lucky number?**	**11. Sentence Dictation** (See page 122) **Can a goat give birth to piglets?** **The skirt was too long.** **Jogging makes me thirsty.** **Is thirteen a lucky number?** After writing, children read back sounds, words and sentences.

Snappy Lesson 40 *FastTrack*

STEP 3.1

Review: Sound /er/ written as er, ur, ir

Learning Objectives: to review a set of letter/sound correspondences; to learn the main ways of spelling the sound /er/, read these spelling choices in words and sentences and write them in dictated words and sentences.

Example grid:

er	ur	ir
her	fur	girl
fern	burn	bird
term	turn	sir
herd	urn	shirt
herbs	hurt	third
stern	surf	first

1. Draw a blank three-column grid on the board and explain that the group will be finding the main ways that the sound /er/ can be written down.

2. Show the flashcard for /er/ and ask children the main ways of writing the /er/ sound. They may use letter names. Write the graphemes at the top of the columns on the grid.

3. Ask the children to say a word that contains the sound /er/ and then to say which column it goes into. Write the choice in the correct column.

4. Ask the children to continue to generate examples while you write them in the correct column. There are some examples shown in the grid above if the children need prompting. Keep going until the columns are full.

5. Ask one child to come to the board, read the words in that column, underline the pattern, and comment on the position of the alternative spelling pattern in the word (i.e. beginning, middle or end).

6. Ask children to come to the board in turn until all of the alternative spelling patterns have been read, underlined and the position of the alternative spelling pattern commented on.

7. Children copy the grid into their books. Explain that they can add to this over time. Alternatively, make copies of the grid (see page 123) and stick these into the children's books. Explain that the words in this grid may not be exactly the same as those the children came up with.

8. Remove the grid from the board and dictate words (see example grid above) and the following sentences to the group for them to write down on a clean page or mini-whiteboard.

   Her teacher this term is stern.
   She has burned her fur coat.
   The girl wants a pet bird.

9. After writing the dictation, ask the children to read back a selection of words and sentences. Check for correct spelling choices and punctuation.

10. Ask the children to write a sentence of their own, using one of the words they have encountered. Listen to the children say the sentences aloud first. Moderate grammar and check for correct spelling choices and punctuation.

Snappy Lesson 41

STEP 3.1

Sound /or/ written as or

Learning Objectives: to learn the main ways of spelling the sound /or/; to blend and segment words and sentences containing or

Success Criteria: to read words and sentences containing or spelling of sound /or/ and write dictated words and sentences with 100% accuracy

Reading	Spelling
1. Review Sounds (show as pack) • er ur ir	**7. Write Sounds** • er ur ir
2. Spelling: or Show the flashcard for **or**. Then with all the phonemes play the **Grab Game**. With the cards on the table, say a sound and ask the children to 'grab' for the letter. **Fingertips Freeze** when they touch the flashcard. Only allow one 'grab'.	**8. Spelling: or** Model writing the letters on the board and talk through letter formation from exit stroke of first letter to start point of the next letter for joined-up writing. **Sky Write** the letters together. Ask children to write the sound on their whiteboards or paper. Check the letter formation for the correct start points, exit strokes and place on the line.
3. Oral Blending (Robot Game) Play the **Robot Game**. Pretend to be a Robot who can only speak in sounds (robot speech), moving arms back and forth like robot arms, in time with each sound. • Say the sounds **p-or-k**, ask children to listen and say the word. • Repeat for: **thorn, north, short**	**9. Oral Segmenting (Phoneme Fingers)** Say a word and the children use **Phoneme Fingers** to flick their fingers for each sound in: • **p-or-k, th-or-n, n-or-th, sh-or-t**
4. Manipulating (Swap) Sounds Stick vowel cards at the top of the board: **i or ur**. Stick consonant cards at the bottom: **b c f k m n ng** Play the **Full Circle Word Game** using the letters on the board to make a word. Ask the children to use **Phoneme Fingers** for each sound in the word. Read the word to the children. Ask a child to change one or more sounds in the word, swapping card/s from the word with card/s at either the bottom or the top of the board. Use **Phoneme Fingers** to make and read the new word. Continue the game changing one sound at a time until you get back to the first word made. **Full circle words: or, for, fork, cork, corn, morn, morning, born, burn, fur, for, or**	
5. Reading Words Ask children to read these words: • pork, thorn, north, short	**10. Word Dictation** Ask children to tap for the sounds and write: • pork, thorn, north, short
6. Reading Sentences (See page 123) Pork comes from a pig. Do tulips have thorns? A north wind is cold. Her fur coat was short.	**11. Sentence Dictation** (See page 123) Pork comes from a pig. Do tulips have thorns? A north wind is cold. Her fur coat was short. After writing, children read back sounds, words and sentences.

Snappy Lesson 42

STEP 3.1

Sound /or/ written as au

Learning Objectives: to learn the main ways of spelling the sound /or/; to blend and segment words and sentences containing au

Success Criteria: to read words and sentences containing au spelling of sound /or/ and write dictated words and sentences with 100% accuracy

Reading	Spelling
1. Review Sounds (show as pack) • er ur ir or	**8. Write Sounds** • er ur ir or
2. New Spelling: au Show the flashcard for **au**. Then with all the phonemes play the **Grab Game**. With the cards on the table, say a sound and ask the children to 'grab' for the letter. **Fingertips Freeze** when they touch the flashcard. Only allow one 'grab'.	**9. New Spelling: au** Model writing the letters on the board and talk through letter formation from exit stroke of first letter to start point of the next letter for joined-up writing. **Sky Write** the letters together. Ask children to write the sound on their whiteboards or paper. Check the letter formation for the correct start points, exit strokes and place on the line.
3. Oral Blending (Robot Game) Play the **Robot Game**. Pretend to be a Robot who can only speak in sounds (robot speech), moving arms back and forth like robot arms, in time with each sound. • Say the sounds **f-au-l-t**, ask children to listen and say the word. • Repeat for: **cauldron, August**	**10. Oral Segmenting (Phoneme Fingers)** Say a word and the children use **Phoneme Fingers** to flick their fingers for each sound in: • **f-au-l-t, c-au-l-d-r-o-n, Au-g-u-s-t**

4. Manipulating (Swap) Sounds

Stick vowel cards at the top of the board: **or au**. Stick consonant cards at the bottom: **f h k l n p t**

Play the **Full Circle Word Game** using the letters on the board to make a word. Ask the children to use **Phoneme Fingers** for each sound in the word. Read the word to the children. Ask a child to change one or more sounds in the word, swapping card/s from the word with card/s at either the bottom or the top of the board. Use **Phoneme Fingers** to make and read the new word. Continue the game changing one sound at a time until you get back to the first word made.

Full circle words: pork, Paul, haul, haunt, fault, faun, fork, pork

5. Reading Words Ask children to read these words: • **fault, cauldron, August**	**11. Word Dictation** Ask children to tap for the sounds and write: • **fault, cauldron, August**
6. Reading Tricky Words: autumn • Show flashcard with the tricky bit underlined. • Together, with the children, sound and say the word using the known letter/sound matches. • Point out that the word doesn't sound like this, identify the tricky bit, and provide tricky sound: the 'mn' sounds /m/. • Sound and say the word correctly together.	**12. Tricky Words Dictation: autumn** • Say the tricky word and remind children to watch out for the tricky bit. • Ask children to say the word, tap for the sounds and write each grapheme. Model with **Phoneme Fingers**, if necessary.
7. Reading Sentences (See page 123) The crash was not my fault. The wizard stirs his cauldron. I might visit you in August. Harvest supper is held in autumn.	**13. Sentence Dictation** (See page 123) The crash was not my fault. The wizard stirs his cauldron. I might visit you in August. Harvest supper is held in autumn. After writing, children read back sounds, words and sentences.

Snappy Lesson 43

STEP 3.1

Sound /or/ written as aw

Learning Objectives: to learn the main ways of spelling the sound /or/; to blend and segment words and sentences containing aw

Success Criteria: to read words and sentences containing aw spelling of sound /or/ and write dictated words and sentences with 100% accuracy

Reading	Spelling
1. Review Sounds (show as pack) • er ur ir or au	**7. Write Sounds** • er ur ir or au
2. New Spelling: aw Show the flashcard for **aw**. Then with all the phonemes play the **Grab Game**. With the cards on the table, say a sound and ask the children to 'grab' for the letter. **Fingertips Freeze** when they touch the flashcard. Only allow one 'grab'.	**8. New Spelling: aw** Model writing the letters on the board and talk through letter formation from exit stroke of first letter to start point of the next letter for joined-up writing. **Sky Write** the letters together. Ask children to write the sound on their whiteboards or paper. Check the letter formation for the correct start points, exit strokes and place on the line.
3. Oral Blending (Robot Game) Play the **Robot Game**. Pretend to be a Robot who can only speak in sounds (robot speech), moving arms back and forth like robot arms, in time with each sound. • Say the sounds **y-aw-n**, ask children to listen and say the word. • Repeat for: **prawn, straw, drawer**	**9. Oral Segmenting (Phoneme Fingers)** Say a word and the children use **Phoneme Fingers** to flick their fingers for each sound in: • **y-aw-n, p-r-aw-n, s-t-r-aw, d-r-aw-er**

4. Manipulating (Swap) Sounds
Stick vowel cards at the top of the board: **or au aw**
Stick consonant cards at the bottom: **j l n p r s t**

Play the **Full Circle Word Game** using the letters on the board to make a word. Ask the children to use **Phoneme Fingers** for each sound in the word. Read the word to the children. Ask a child to change one or more sounds in the word, swapping card/s from the word with card/s at either the bottom or the top of the board. Use **Phoneme Fingers** to make and read the new word. Continue the game changing one sound at a time until you get back to the first word made.

Full circle words: pawn, Paul, port, sort, saw, paw, raw, jaw, lawn, pawn

5. Reading Words Ask children to read these words: • **yawn, prawn, straw, drawer**	**10. Word Dictation** Ask children to tap for the sounds and write: • **yawn, prawn, straw, drawer**
6. Reading Sentences (See page 124) I tried not to yawn. Is prawn salad on the menu? The foal lay on dry straw. She found her card in the drawer.	**11. Sentence Dictation** (See page 124) I tried not to yawn. Is prawn salad on the menu? The foal lay on dry straw. She found her card in the drawer. After writing, children read back sounds, words and sentences.

Snappy Lesson 44

STEP 3.1

Sound /or/ written as al

Learning Objectives: to learn the main ways of spelling the sound /or/; to blend and segment words and sentences containing al

Success Criteria: to read words and sentences containing al spelling of sound /or/ and write dictated words and sentences with 100% accuracy

Reading	Spelling
1. Review Sounds (show as pack) • er ur ir or au aw	**7. Write Sounds** • er ur ir or au aw
2. New Spelling: al Show the flashcard for **al**. Then with all the phonemes play the **Grab Game**. With the cards on the table, say a sound and ask the children to 'grab' for the letter. **Fingertips Freeze** when they touch the flashcard. Only allow one 'grab'.	**8. New Spelling: al** Model writing the letters on the board and talk through letter formation from exit stroke of first letter to start point of the next letter for joined-up writing. **Sky Write** the letters together. Ask children to write the sound on their whiteboards or paper. Check the letter formation for the correct start points, exit strokes and place on the line.
3. Oral Blending (Robot Game) Play the **Robot Game**. Pretend to be a Robot who can only speak in sounds (robot speech), moving arms back and forth like robot arms, in time with each sound. • Say the sounds **w-al-l**, ask children to listen and say the word. • Repeat for: **fall, small, football**	**9. Oral Segmenting (Phoneme Fingers)** Say a word and the children use **Phoneme Fingers** to flick their fingers for each sound in: • w-al-l, f-al-l, s-m-al-l, f-oo-t-b-al-l

4. Manipulating (Swap) Sounds

Stick vowel cards at the top of the board: **or au aw al**
Stick consonant cards at the bottom: **b c h l m n r s**

Play the **Full Circle Word Game** using the letters on the board to make a word. Ask the children to use **Phoneme Fingers** for each sound in the word. Read the word to the children. Ask a child to change one or more sounds in the word, swapping card/s from the word with card/s at either the bottom or the top of the board. Use **Phoneme Fingers** to make and read the new word. Continue the game changing one sound at a time until you get back to the first word made.

Full circle words: call, crawl, raw, saw, haw, haul, hall, horn, born, brawn, raw, maul, mall, call

| **5. Reading Words**
Ask children to read these words:
• **wall, fall, small, football** | **10. Word Dictation**
Ask children to tap for the sounds and write:
• **wall, fall, small, football** |
| **6. Reading Sentences** (See page 124)
The stone wall is five feet high.
The fall hurt his leg.
The small kitten is cute.
Do you like to play football? | **11. Sentence Dictation** (See page 124)
The stone wall is five feet high.
The fall hurt his leg.
The small kitten is cute.
Do you like to play football?

After writing, children read back sounds, words and sentences. |

Snappy Lesson 45 *FastTrack*

STEP 3.1

Review: Sound /or/ written as or, au, aw, al

Learning Objectives: to review a set of letter/sound correspondences; to learn the main ways of spelling the sound /or/, read these spelling choices in words and sentences and write them in dictated words and sentences.

Example grid:

or	au	aw	al
for	Paul	saw	all
fork	haul	paw	ball
sort	launch	raw	talk
horse	haunted	jaw	walk
storm	August	law	call
forbid	automatic	shawl	beanstalk

1. Draw a blank four-column grid on the board and explain that the group will be finding the main ways that the sound /or/ can be written down.

2. Show the flashcard for /or/ and ask children the main ways of writing the /or/ sound. They may use letter names. Write the graphemes at the top of the columns on the grid.

3. Ask the children to say a word that contains the sound /or/ and then to say which column it goes into. Write the choice in the correct column.

4. Ask the children to continue to generate examples while you write them in the correct column. There are some examples shown in the grid above if the children need prompting. Keep going until the columns are full.

5. Ask one child to come to the board, read the words in that column, underline the pattern, and comment on the position of the alternative spelling pattern in the word (i.e. beginning, middle or end).

6. Ask children to come to the board in turn until all of the alternative spelling patterns have been read, underlined and the position of the alternative spelling pattern commented on.

7. Children copy the grid into their books. Explain that they can add to this over time. Alternatively, make copies of the grid (see page 124) and stick these into the children's books. Explain that the words in this grid may not be exactly the same as those the children came up with.

8. Remove the grid from the board and dictate words (see example grid above) and the following sentences to the group for them to write down on a clean page or mini-whiteboard.

    Can you sort out the forks and spoons for me?
    Paul went to a haunted house in August.
    I saw that the dog's paw and jaw were hurt.
    We can play with the ball as we walk and talk.

9. After writing the dictation, ask the children to read back a selection of words and sentences. Check for correct spelling choices and punctuation.

10. Ask the children to write a sentence of their own, using one of the words they have encountered. Listen to the children say the sentences aloud first. Moderate grammar and check for correct spelling choices and punctuation.

Snappy Lesson 46

STEP 3.1

Sound /oi/ written as oi

Learning Objectives: to learn the main ways of spelling the sound /oi/; to blend and segment words and sentences containing oi

Success Criteria: to read words and sentences containing oi spelling of sound /oi/ and write dictated words and sentences with 100% accuracy

Reading	Spelling
1. Review Sounds (show as pack) • or au aw al	**8. Write Sounds** • or au aw al
2. Spelling: oi Show the flashcard for **oi**. Then with all the phonemes play the **Grab Game**. With the cards on the table, say a sound and ask the children to 'grab' for the letter. **Fingertips Freeze** when they touch the flashcard. Only allow one 'grab'.	**9. Spelling: oi** Model writing the letters on the board and talk through letter formation from exit stroke of first letter to start point of the next letter for joined-up writing. **Sky Write** the letters together. Ask children to write the sound on their whiteboards or paper. Check the letter formation for the correct start points, exit strokes and place on the line.
3. Oral Blending (Robot Game) Play the **Robot Game**. Pretend to be a Robot who can only speak in sounds (robot speech), moving arms back and forth like robot arms, in time with each sound. • Say the sounds **c-oi-l**, ask children to listen and say the word. • Repeat for: **point, spoil, moist**	**10. Oral Segmenting (Phoneme Fingers)** Say a word and the children use **Phoneme Fingers** to flick their fingers for each sound in: • **c-oi-l, p-oi-n-t, s-p-oi-l, m-oi-s-t**
4. Manipulating (Swap) Sounds Stick vowel cards at the top of the board: **oi**. Stick consonant cards at the bottom: **b c j n p s t l** Play the **Full Circle Word Game** using the letters on the board to make a word. Ask the children to use **Phoneme Fingers** for each sound in the word. Read the word to the children. Ask a child to change one or more sounds in the word, swapping card/s from the word with card/s at either the bottom or the top of the board. Use **Phoneme Fingers** to make and read the new word. Continue the game changing one sound at a time until you get back to the first word made. **Full circle words: join, joint, point, coin, coil, boil, soil, coil, coin, join**	
5. Reading Words Ask children to read these words: • **coil, point, spoil, moist**	**11. Word Dictation** Ask children to tap for the sounds and write: • **coil, point, spoil, moist**
6. Reading Tricky Words: ag<u>ai</u>n • Show flashcard with the tricky bit underlined. • Together, with the children, sound and say the word using the known letter/sound matches. • Point out that the word doesn't sound like this, identify the tricky bit, and provide tricky sound: the 'ai' sounds /e/. • Sound and say the word correctly together.	**12. Tricky Words Dictation: ag<u>ai</u>n** • Say the tricky word and remind children to watch out for the tricky bit. • Ask children to say the word, tap for the sounds and write each grapheme. Model with **Phoneme Fingers**, if necessary.
7. Reading Sentences (See page 125) **The snake looks like a coil of rope.** **A dart has a sharp point.** **Will garlic spoil the taste of cake again?** **Is the beef moist or dry?**	**13. Sentence Dictation** (See page 125) **The snake looks like a coil of rope.** **A dart has a sharp point.** **Will garlic spoil the taste of cake again?** **Is the beef moist or dry?** After writing, children read back sounds, words and sentences.

Snappy Lesson 47

STEP 3.1

Sound /oi/ written as oy

Learning Objectives: to learn the main ways of spelling the sound /oi/; to blend and segment words and sentences containing oy

Success Criteria: to read words and sentences containing oy spelling of sound /oi/ and write dictated words and sentences with 100% accuracy

Reading	Spelling

1. Review Sounds (show as pack)
- or au aw al oi

7. Write Sounds
- or au aw al oi

2. New Spelling: oy
Show the flashcard for **oy**. Then with all the phonemes play the **Grab Game**. With the cards on the table, say a sound and ask the children to 'grab' for the letter. **Fingertips Freeze** when they touch the flashcard. Only allow one 'grab'.

8. New Spelling: oy
Model writing the letters on the board and talk through letter formation from exit stroke of first letter to start point of the next letter for joined-up writing. **Sky Write** the letters together. Ask children to write the sound on their whiteboards or paper. Check the letter formation for the correct start points, exit strokes and place on the line.

3. Oral Blending (Robot Game)
Play the **Robot Game**. Pretend to be a Robot who can only speak in sounds (robot speech), moving arms back and forth like robot arms, in time with each sound.
- Say the sounds **t-oy**, ask children to listen and say the word.
- Repeat for: **boy, annoy, destroy**

9. Oral Segmenting (Phoneme Fingers)
Say a word and the children use **Phoneme Fingers** to flick their fingers for each sound in:
- **t-oy, b-oy, a-n/n-oy, d-e-s-t-r-oy**

4. Manipulating (Swap) Sounds
Stick vowel cards at the top of the board: **oi oy**. Stick consonant cards at the bottom: **b c j l n t**

Play the **Full Circle Word Game** using the letters on the board to make a word. Ask the children to use **Phoneme Fingers** for each sound in the word. Read the word to the children. Ask a child to change one or more sounds in the word, swapping card/s from the word with card/s at either the bottom or the top of the board. Use **Phoneme Fingers** to make and read the new word. Continue the game changing one sound at a time until you get back to the first word made.

Full circle words: boy, boil, toil, toy, joy, join, coin, coy, boy

5. Reading Words
Ask children to read these words:
- **toy, boy, annoy, destroy**

10. Word Dictation
Ask children to tap for the sounds and write:
- **toy, boy, annoy, destroy**

6. Reading Sentences (See page 125)
The children broke the toy.
The boy plays outside.
Loud sounds annoy us.
Locusts can destroy crops.

11. Sentence Dictation (See page 125)
The children broke the toy.
The boy plays outside.
Loud sounds annoy us.
Locusts can destroy crops.

After writing, children read back sounds, words and sentences.

Snappy Lesson 48 *FastTrack*

STEP 3.1

Review: Sound /oi/ written as oi, oy

Learning Objectives: to review a set of letter/sound correspondences; to learn the main ways of spelling the sound /oi/, read these spelling choices in words and sentences and write them in dictated words and sentences.

Example grid:

oi	oy
oil	boy
boil	toy
coins	joy
join	oyster
soil	royal
moist	enjoy

1. Draw a blank two-column grid on the board and explain that the group will be finding the main ways that the sound /oi/ can be written down.

2. Show the flashcard for /oi and ask children the main ways of writing the /oi/ sound. They may use letter names. Write the graphemes at the top of the columns on the grid.

3. Ask the children to say a word that contains the sound /oi/ and then to say which column it goes into. Write the choice in the correct column.

4. Ask the children to continue to generate examples while you write them in the correct column. There are some examples shown in the grid above if the children need prompting. Keep going until the columns are full.

5. Ask one child to come to the board, read the words in that column, underline the pattern, and comment on the position of the alternative spelling pattern in the word (i.e. beginning, middle or end).

6. Ask children to come to the board in turn until all of the alternative spelling patterns have been read, underlined and the position of the alternative spelling pattern commented on.

7. Children copy the grid into their books. Explain that they can add to this over time. Alternatively, make copies of the grid (see page 125) and stick these into the children's books. Explain that the words in this grid may not be exactly the same as those the children came up with.

8. Remove the grid from the board and dictate words (see example grid above) and the following sentences to the group for them to write down on a clean page or mini-whiteboard.

    If you boil the joint of beef you will spoil it.
    The boy's toy train gave him so much joy.

9. After writing the dictation, ask the children to read back a selection of words and sentences. Check for correct spelling choices and punctuation.

10. Ask the children to write a sentence of their own, using one of the words they have encountered. Listen to the children say the sentences aloud first. Moderate grammar and check for correct spelling choices and punctuation.

Snappy Lesson 49

STEP 3.1

Sound /ou/ written as ou

Learning Objectives: to learn the main ways of spelling the sound /ou/; to blend and segment words and sentences containing ou

Success Criteria: to read words and sentences containing ou spelling of sound /ou/ and write dictated words and sentences with 100% accuracy

Reading	Spelling
1. Review Sounds (show as pack) • oi oy	**7. Write Sounds** • oi oy
2. Spelling: ou Show the flashcard for **ou**. Then with all the phonemes play the **Grab Game**. With the cards on the table, say a sound and ask the children to 'grab' for the letter. **Fingertips Freeze** when they touch the flashcard. Only allow one 'grab'.	**8. Spelling: ou** Model writing the letters on the board and talk through letter formation from exit stroke of first letter to start point of the next letter for joined-up writing. **Sky Write** the letters together. Ask children to write the sound on their whiteboards or paper. Check the letter formation for the correct start points, exit strokes and place on the line.
3. Oral Blending (Robot Game) Play the **Robot Game**. Pretend to be a Robot who can only speak in sounds (robot speech), moving arms back and forth like robot arms, in time with each sound. • Say the sounds **c-l-ou-d**, ask children to listen and say the word. • Repeat for: **proud, round, shout**	**9. Oral Segmenting (Phoneme Fingers)** Say a word and the children use **Phoneme Fingers** to flick their fingers for each sound in: • **c-l-ou-d, p-r-ou-d, r-ou-n-d, sh-ou-t**
4. Manipulating (Swap) Sounds Stick vowel cards at the top of the board: **a ou**. Stick consonant cards at the bottom: **b c d f l n p r s t** Play the **Full Circle Word Game** using the letters on the board to make a word. Ask the children to use **Phoneme Fingers** for each sound in the word. Read the word to the children. Ask a child to change one or more sounds in the word, swapping card/s from the word with card/s at either the bottom or the top of the board. Use **Phoneme Fingers** to make and read the new word. Continue the game changing one sound at a time until you get back to the first word made. **Full circle words:** loud, cloud, proud, round, sound, found, bound, bout, about, sprout, proud, loud	
5. Reading Words Ask children to read these words: • **cloud, proud, round, shout**	**10. Word Dictation** Ask children to tap for the sounds and write: • **cloud, proud, round, shout**
6. Reading Sentences (See page 126) The sun went behind a cloud. The teacher was proud of her class. Turn round and look this way. There is no need to shout.	**11. Sentence Dictation** (See page 126) The sun went behind a cloud. The teacher was proud of her class. Turn round and look this way. There is no need to shout. After writing, children read back sounds, words and sentences.

# Snappy Lesson 50

STEP 3.1

Sound /ou/ written as ow

Learning Objectives: to learn the main ways of spelling the sound /ou/; to blend and segment words and sentences containing ow

Success Criteria: to read words and sentences containing ow spelling of sound /ou/ and write dictated words and sentences with 100% accuracy

Reading	Spelling
1. Review Sounds (show as pack) • oi oy ou	**7. Write Sounds** • oi oy ou
2. New Spelling: OW Show the flashcard for **ow**. Then with all the phonemes play the **Grab Game**. With the cards on the table, say a sound and ask the children to 'grab' for the letter. **Fingertips Freeze** when they touch the flashcard. Only allow one 'grab'.	**8. New Spelling: OW** Model writing the letters on the board and talk through letter formation from exit stroke of first letter to start point of the next letter for joined-up writing. **Sky Write** the letters together. Ask children to write the sound on their whiteboards or paper. Check the letter formation for the correct start points, exit strokes and place on the line.
3. Oral Blending (Robot Game) Play the **Robot Game**. Pretend to be a Robot who can only speak in sounds (robot speech), moving arms back and forth like robot arms, in time with each sound. • Say the sounds **c-ow**, ask children to listen and say the word. • Repeat for: **town, clown, brown**	**9. Oral Segmenting (Phoneme Fingers)** Say a word and the children use **Phoneme Fingers** to flick their fingers for each sound in: • **c-ow, t-ow-n, c-l-ow-n, b-r-ow-n**

4. Manipulating (Swap) Sounds

Stick vowel cards at the top of the board: **ou ow**. Stick consonant cards at the bottom: **b c d g l n r w**

Play the **Full Circle Word Game** using the letters on the board to make a word. Ask the children to use **Phoneme Fingers** for each sound in the word. Read the word to the children. Ask a child to change one or more sounds in the word, swapping card/s from the word with card/s at either the bottom or the top of the board. Use **Phoneme Fingers** to make and read the new word. Continue the game changing one sound at a time until you get back to the first word made.

Full circle words: owl, cowl, gown, ground, round, brown, brow, row, now, wow, owl

5. Reading Words Ask children to read these words: • **cow, town, clown, brown**	**10. Word Dictation** Ask children to tap for the sounds and write: • **cow, town, clown, brown**
6. Reading Sentences (See page 126) The farmer keeps cows and horses. Gran took a bus to the town. The clown had a sad mouth. Shall I paint the wall brown?	**11. Sentence Dictation** (See page 126) The farmer keeps cows and horses. Gran took a bus to the town. The clown had a sad mouth. Shall I paint the wall brown? After writing, children read back sounds, words and sentences.

Snappy Lesson 51 *FastTrack*

STEP 3.1

Review: Sound /ou/ written as ou, ow

Learning Objectives: to review a set of letter/sound correspondences; to learn the main ways of spelling the sound /ou/, read these spelling choices in words and sentences and write them in dictated words and sentences.

Example grid:

ou	ow
out	now
about	down
cloud	owl
found	cow
ground	how
loudest	town

1. Draw a blank two-column grid on the board and explain that the group will be finding the main ways that the sound /ou/ can be written down.

2. Show the flashcard for /ou/ and ask children the main ways of writing the /ou/ sound. They may use letter names. Write the graphemes at the top of the columns on the grid.

3. Ask the children to say a word that contains the sound /ou/ and then to say which column it goes into. Write the choice in the correct column.

4. Ask the children to continue to generate examples while you write them in the correct column. There are some examples shown in the grid above if the children need prompting. Keep going until the columns are full.

5. Ask one child to come to the board, read the words in that column, underline the pattern, and comment on the position of the alternative spelling pattern in the word (i.e. beginning, middle or end).

6. Ask children to come to the board in turn until all of the alternative spelling patterns have been read, underlined and the position of the alternative spelling pattern commented on.

7. Children copy the grid into their books. Explain that they can add to this over time. Alternatively, make copies of the grid (see page 126) and stick these into the children's books. Explain that the words in this grid may not be exactly the same as those the children came up with.

8. Remove the grid from the board and dictate words (see example grid above) and the following sentences to the group for them to write down on a clean page or mini-whiteboard.

   We played loud games out on the playground. Sit down now, before you go to town.

9. After writing the dictation, ask the children to read back a selection of words and sentences. Check for correct spelling choices and punctuation.

10. Ask the children to write a sentence of their own, using one of the words they have encountered. Listen to the children say the sentences aloud first. Moderate grammar and check for correct spelling choices and punctuation.

Snappy Lesson 52

STEP 3.1

Sound /oo/ written as oo

Learning Objectives: to learn the main ways of spelling the sound /oo/; to blend and segment words and sentences containing oo

Success Criteria: to read words and sentences containing oo spelling of sound /oo/ and write dictated words and sentences with 100% accuracy

Reading	Spelling
1. Review Sounds (show as pack) • ou ow	**8. Write Sounds** • ou ow
2. Spelling: oo Show the flashcard for **oo**. Then with all the phonemes play the **Grab Game**. With the cards on the table, say a sound and ask the children to 'grab' for the letter. **Fingertips Freeze** when they touch the flashcard. Only allow one 'grab'.	**9. Spelling: oo** Model writing the letters on the board and talk through letter formation from exit stroke of first letter to start point of the next letter for joined-up writing. **Sky Write** the letters together. Ask children to write the sound on their whiteboards or paper. Check the letter formation for the correct start points, exit strokes and place on the line.
3. Oral Blending (Robot Game) Play the **Robot Game**. Pretend to be a Robot who can only speak in sounds (robot speech), moving arms back and forth like robot arms, in time with each sound. • Say the sounds **l-oo-k**, ask children to listen and say the word. • Repeat for: **book, wood, wool**	**10. Oral Segmenting (Phoneme Fingers)** Say a word and the children use **Phoneme Fingers** to flick their fingers for each sound in: • **l-oo-k, b-oo-k, w-oo-d, w-oo-l**
4. Manipulating (Swap) Sounds Stick vowel cards at the top of the board: **ai oo**. Stick consonant cards at the bottom: **b c d g k r s t w** Play the **Full Circle Word Game** using the letters on the board to make a word. Ask the children to use **Phoneme Fingers** for each sound in the word. Read the word to the children. Ask a child to change one or more sounds in the word, swapping card/s from the word with card/s at either the bottom or the top of the board. Use **Phoneme Fingers** to make and read the new word. Continue the game changing one sound at a time until you get back to the first word made. **Full circle words: good, book, bait, wait, wood, stood, staid, raid, rook, cook, good**	
5. Reading Words Ask children to read these words: • **look, book, wood, wool**	**11. Word Dictation** Ask children to tap for the sounds and write: • **look, book, wood, wool**
6. Reading Tricky Words: I'<u>ve</u> • Show flashcard with the tricky bit underlined. • Together, with the children, sound and say the word using the known letter/sound matches. • Point out that the word doesn't sound like this, identify the tricky bit, and provide tricky sound: the 've' sounds /v/. The apostrophe replaces the 'ha' of 'have'. • Sound and say the word correctly together.	**12. Tricky Words Dictation: I'<u>ve</u>** • Say the tricky word and remind children to watch out for the tricky bit. • Ask children to say the word, tap for the sounds and write each grapheme. Model with **Phoneme Fingers**, if necessary.
7. Reading Sentences (See page 127) I've looked for my coat. I need to find the book. Can you chop wood with a spade? We get wool from sheep.	**13. Sentence Dictation** (See page 127) I've looked for my coat. I need to find the book. Can you chop wood with a spade? We get wool from sheep. After writing, children read back sounds, words and sentences.

Snappy Lesson 53

STEP 3.1

Sound /oo/ written as oul

Learning Objectives: to learn the main ways of spelling the sound /oo/; to blend and segment words and sentences containing oul

Success Criteria: to read words and sentences containing oul spelling of sound /oo/ and write dictated words and sentences with 100% accuracy

Reading	Spelling
1. Review Sounds (show as pack) • ou ow oo	**7. Write Sounds** • ou ow oo
2. New Spelling: oul Show the flashcard for **oul**. Then with all the phonemes play the **Grab Game**. With the cards on the table, say a sound and ask the children to 'grab' for the letter. **Fingertips Freeze** when they touch the flashcard. Only allow one 'grab'.	**8. New Spelling: oul** Model writing the letters on the board and talk through letter formation from exit stroke of first letter to start point of the next letter for joined-up writing. **Sky Write** the letters together. Ask children to write the sound on their whiteboards or paper. Check the letter formation for the correct start points, exit strokes and place on the line.
3. Oral Blending (Robot Game) Play the **Robot Game**. Pretend to be a Robot who can only speak in sounds (robot speech), moving arms back and forth like robot arms, in time with each sound. • Say the sounds **w-oul-d**, ask children to listen and say the word. • Repeat for: **could, should**	**9. Oral Segmenting (Phoneme Fingers)** Say a word and the children use **Phoneme Fingers** to flick their fingers for each sound in: • **w-oul-d, c-oul-d, sh-oul-d**

4. Manipulating (Swap) Sounds

Stick vowel cards at the top of the board: **oo oul**. Stick consonant cards at the bottom: **c d w sh**

Play the **Full Circle Word Game** using the letters on the board to make a word. Ask the children to use **Phoneme Fingers** for each sound in the word. Read the word to the children. Ask a child to change one or more sounds in the word, swapping card/s from the word with card/s at either the bottom or the top of the board. Use **Phoneme Fingers** to make and read the new word. Continue the game changing one sound at a time until you get back to the first word made.

Full circle words: wood, would, could, should, shook, wood

5. Reading Words Ask children to read these words: • **would, could, should**	**10. Word Dictation** Ask children to tap for the sounds and write: • **would, could, should**
6. Reading Sentences (See page 127) **Would you like a cup of tea?** **Could you come to my party?** **I should try harder.**	**11. Sentence Dictation** (See page 127) **Would you like a cup of tea?** **Could you come to my party?** **I should try harder.** After writing, children read back sounds, words and sentences.

Snappy Lesson 54

STEP 3.1

Sound /oo/ written as u

Learning Objectives: to learn the main ways of spelling the sound /oo/; to blend and segment words and sentences containing u

Success Criteria: to read words and sentences containing u spelling of sound /oo/ and write dictated words and sentences with 100% accuracy

Reading	Spelling
1. Review Sounds (show as pack) • ou ow oo oul	**7. Write Sounds** • ou ow oo oul
2. New Spelling: u Show the flashcard for **u**. Then with all the phonemes play the **Grab Game**. With the cards on the table, say a sound and ask the children to 'grab' for the letter. **Fingertips Freeze** when they touch the flashcard. Only allow one 'grab'.	**8. New Spelling: u** Model writing the letter on the board and talk through letter formation. **Sky Write** the letter together. Ask children to write the sound on their whiteboards or paper. Check the letter formation for the correct start point, exit stroke and place on the line.
3. Oral Blending (Robot Game) Play the **Robot Game**. Pretend to be a Robot who can only speak in sounds (robot speech), moving arms back and forth like robot arms, in time with each sound. • Say the sounds **p-u-t**, ask children to listen and say the word. • Repeat for: **push, pull, playful**	**9. Oral Segmenting (Phoneme Fingers)** Say a word and the children use **Phoneme Fingers** to flick their fingers for each sound in: • **p-u-t, p-u-sh, p-u-ll, p-l-ay-f-u-l**

4. Manipulating (Swap) Sounds

Stick vowel cards at the top of the board: **ou oo oul u**
Stick consonant cards at the bottom: **c d f ll p t w sh**

Play the **Full Circle Word Game** using the letters on the board to make a word. Ask the children to use **Phoneme Fingers** for each sound in the word. Read the word to the children. Ask a child to change one or more sounds in the word, swapping card/s from the word with card/s at either the bottom or the top of the board. Use **Phoneme Fingers** to make and read the new word. Continue the game changing one sound at a time until you get back to the first word made.

Full circle words: foot, could, would, should, shout, pout, put, push, pull, full, foot

5. Reading Words Ask children to read these words: • put, push, pull, playful	**10. Word Dictation** Ask children to tap for the sounds and write: • put, push, pull, playful
6. Reading Sentences (See page 127) He put on his shirt. Help me push the pram. You need to pull out the weeds. The puppy is playful.	**11. Sentence Dictation** (See page 127) He put on his shirt. Help me push the pram. You need to pull out the weeds. The puppy is playful. After writing, children read back sounds, words and sentences.

Snappy Lesson 55 *FastTrack*

STEP 3.1

Review: Sound /oo/ written as oo, oul, u

Learning Objectives: to review a set of letter/sound correspondences; to learn the main ways of spelling the sound /oo/, read these spelling choices in words and sentences and write them in dictated words and sentences.

Example grid:

oo	oul	u
look	could	put
foot	would	pull
cook	should	push
good		full
book		bush
stood		playful

1. Draw a blank three-column grid on the board and explain that the group will be finding the main ways that the sound /oo/ can be written down.

2. Show the flashcard for /oo/ and ask children the main ways of writing the /oo/ sound. They may use letter names. Write the graphemes at the top of the columns on the grid.

3. Ask the children to say a word that contains the sound /oo/ and then to say which column it goes into. Write the choice in the correct column.

4. Ask the children to continue to generate examples while you write them in the correct column. There are some examples shown in the grid above if the children need prompting. Keep going until the columns are full.

5. Ask one child to come to the board, read the words in that column, underline the pattern, and comment on the position of the alternative spelling pattern in the word (i.e. beginning, middle or end).

6. Ask children to come to the board in turn until all of the alternative spelling patterns have been read, underlined and the position of the alternative spelling pattern commented on.

7. Children copy the grid into their books. Explain that they can add to this over time. Alternatively, make copies of the grid (see page 128) and stick these into the children's books. Explain that the words in this grid may not be exactly the same as those the children came up with.

8. Remove the grid from the board and dictate words (see example grid above) and the following sentences to the group for them to write down on a clean page or mini-whiteboard.

   Take a look at my cook books.
   I would eat some more cake if I could, but I should stop now!
   The playful children push and pull their toys.

9. After writing the dictation, ask the children to read back a selection of words and sentences. Check for correct spelling choices and punctuation.

10. Ask the children to write a sentence of their own, using one of the words they have encountered. Listen to the children say the sentences aloud first. Moderate grammar and check for correct spelling choices and punctuation.

Snappy Lesson 56

STEP 3.1

Sound /oo/ written as oo

Learning Objectives: to learn the main ways of spelling the sound /oo/; to blend and segment words and sentences containing oo

Success Criteria: to read words and sentences containing oo spelling of sound /oo/ and write dictated words and sentences with 100% accuracy

Reading	Spelling
1. Review Sounds (show as pack) • oo oul u	**8. Write Sounds** • oo oul u
2. Spelling: oo Show the flashcard for **oo**. Then with all the phonemes play the **Grab Game**. With the cards on the table, say a sound and ask the children to 'grab' for the letter. **Fingertips Freeze** when they touch the flashcard. Only allow one 'grab'.	**9. Spelling: oo** Model writing the letters on the board and talk through letter formation from exit stroke of first letter to start point of the next letter for joined-up writing. **Sky Write** the letters together. Ask children to write the sound on their whiteboards or paper. Check the letter formation for the correct start points, exit strokes and place on the line.
3. Oral Blending (Robot Game) Play the **Robot Game**. Pretend to be a Robot who can only speak in sounds (robot speech), moving arms back and forth like robot arms, in time with each sound. • Say the sounds **t-oo**, ask children to listen and say the word. • Repeat for: **moon, roof, cool**	**10. Oral Segmenting (Phoneme Fingers)** Say a word and the children use **Phoneme Fingers** to flick their fingers for each sound in: • t-oo, m-oo-n, r-oo-f, c-oo-l
4. Manipulating (Swap) Sounds Stick vowel cards at the top of the board: **oo**. Stick consonant cards at the bottom: **b m n r t z** Play the **Full Circle Word Game** using the letters on the board to make a word. Ask the children to use **Phoneme Fingers** for each sound in the word. Read the word to the children. Ask a child to change one or more sounds in the word, swapping card/s from the word with card/s at either the bottom or the top of the board. Use **Phoneme Fingers** to make and read the new word. Continue the game changing one sound at a time until you get back to the first word made. **Full circle words: too, zoo, zoom, room, boom, boot, root, moon, too**	
5. Reading Words Ask children to read these words: • **too, moon, roof, cool**	**11. Word Dictation** Ask children to tap for the sounds and write: • **too, moon, roof, cool**
6. Reading Tricky Words: <u>wh</u>a<u>t</u> • Show flashcard with the tricky bits underlined. • Together, with the children, sound and say the word using the known letter/sound matches. • Point out that the word doesn't sound like this, identify the tricky bits, and provide tricky sounds: the 'wh' sounds /w/ and the 'a' sounds /o/. • Sound and say the word correctly together.	**12. Tricky Words Dictation: <u>wh</u>a<u>t</u>** • Say the tricky word and remind children to watch out for the tricky bits. • Ask children to say the word, tap for the sounds and write each grapheme. Model with **Phoneme Fingers**, if necessary.
7. Reading Sentences (See page 128) I had too much to eat. A cloud went across the moon. The roof needs new tiles. What will cool you down?	**13. Sentence Dictation** (See page 128) I had too much to eat. A cloud went across the moon. The roof needs new tiles. What will cool you down? After writing, children read back sounds, words and sentences.

Snappy Lesson 57

STEP 3.1

Sound /oo/ written as ue

Learning Objectives: to learn the main ways of spelling the sound /oo/; to blend and segment words and sentences containing ue

Success Criteria: to read words and sentences containing ue spelling of sound /oo/ and write dictated words and sentences with 100% accuracy

Reading	Spelling
1. Review Sounds (show as pack) • oo oul u oo	**7. Write Sounds** • oo oul u oo
2. New Spelling: ue Show the flashcard for **ue**. Then with all the phonemes play the **Grab Game**. With the cards on the table, say a sound and ask the children to 'grab' for the letter. **Fingertips Freeze** when they touch the flashcard. Only allow one 'grab'.	**8. New Spelling: ue** Model writing the letters on the board and talk through letter formation from exit stroke of first letter to start point of the next letter for joined-up writing. **Sky Write** the letters together. Ask children to write the sound on their whiteboards or paper. Check the letter formation for the correct start points, exit strokes and place on the line.
3. Oral Blending (Robot Game) Play the **Robot Game**. Pretend to be a Robot who can only speak in sounds (robot speech), moving arms back and forth like robot arms, in time with each sound. • Say the sounds **b-l-ue**, ask children to listen and say the word. • Repeat for: **true, glue, clue**	**9. Oral Segmenting (Phoneme Fingers)** Say a word and the children use **Phoneme Fingers** to flick their fingers for each sound in: • b-l-ue, t-r-ue, g-l-ue, c-l-ue

4. Manipulating (Swap) Sounds

Stick vowel cards at the top of the board: **oo ue**. Stick consonant cards at the bottom: **b c g l r t**

Play the **Full Circle Word Game** using the letters on the board to make a word. Ask the children to use **Phoneme Fingers** for each sound in the word. Read the word to the children. Ask a child to change one or more sounds in the word, swapping card/s from the word with card/s at either the bottom or the top of the board. Use **Phoneme Fingers** to make and read the new word. Continue the game changing one sound at a time until you get back to the first word made.

Full circle words: too, true, blue, glue, clue, cool, coo, too

5. Reading Words Ask children to read these words: • blue, true, glue, clue	**10. Word Dictation** Ask children to tap for the sounds and write: • blue, true, glue, clue
6. Reading Sentences (See page 128) He drives a light blue car. Is it true she came late? Glue can be very sticky. I don't have a clue.	**11. Sentence Dictation** (See page 128) He drives a light blue car. Is it true she came late? Glue can be very sticky. I don't have a clue. After writing, children read back sounds, words and sentences.

Snappy Lesson 58

STEP 3.1

Sound /oo/ written as ew

Learning Objectives: to learn the main ways of spelling the sound /oo/; to blend and segment words and sentences containing ew

Success Criteria: to read words and sentences containing ew spelling of sound /oo/ and write dictated words and sentences with 100% accuracy

Reading	Spelling
1. Review Sounds (show as pack) • oo oul u oo ue	**7. Write Sounds** • oo oul u oo ue
2. New Spelling: ew Show the flashcard for **ew**. Then with all the phonemes play the **Grab Game**. With the cards on the table, say a sound and ask the children to 'grab' for the letter. **Fingertips Freeze** when they touch the flashcard. Only allow one 'grab'.	**8. New Spelling: ew** Model writing the letters on the board and talk through letter formation from exit stroke of first letter to start point of the next letter for joined-up writing. **Sky Write** the letters together. Ask children to write the sound on their whiteboards or paper. Check the letter formation for the correct start points, exit strokes and place on the line.
3. Oral Blending (Robot Game) Play the **Robot Game**. Pretend to be a Robot who can only speak in sounds (robot speech), moving arms back and forth like robot arms, in time with each sound. • Say the sounds **c-r-ew**, ask children to listen and say the word. • Repeat for: **threw, flew, brew**	**9. Oral Segmenting (Phoneme Fingers)** Say a word and the children use **Phoneme Fingers** to flick their fingers for each sound in: • **c-r-ew, th-r-ew, f-l-ew, b-r-ew**

4. Manipulating (Swap) Sounds

Stick vowel cards at the top of the board: **oo ue ew**
Stick consonant cards at the bottom: **b d f g l n r s**

Play the **Full Circle Word Game** using the letters on the board to make a word. Ask the children to use **Phoneme Fingers** for each sound in the word. Read the word to the children. Ask a child to change one or more sounds in the word, swapping card/s from the word with card/s at either the bottom or the top of the board. Use **Phoneme Fingers** to make and read the new word. Continue the game changing one sound at a time until you get back to the first word made.

Full circle words: boo, blue, blew, flew, drew, grew, glue, sue, soon, boon, boo

5. Reading Words Ask children to read these words: • **crew, threw, flew, brew**	**10. Word Dictation** Ask children to tap for the sounds and write: • **crew, threw, flew, brew**
6. Reading Sentences (See page 129) The ship's crew became ill. Paul threw out the rubbish. We flew in a helicopter. Brew the tea in this teapot.	**11. Sentence Dictation** (See page 129) The ship's crew became ill. Paul threw out the rubbish. We flew in a helicopter. Brew the tea in this teapot. After writing, children read back sounds, words and sentences.

Snappy Lesson 59

STEP 3.1

Sound /oo/ written as u-e

Learning Objectives: to learn the main ways of spelling the sound /oo/; to blend and segment words and sentences containing u-e

Success Criteria: to read words and sentences containing u-e spelling of sound /oo/ and write dictated words and sentences with 100% accuracy

Reading	Spelling
1. Review Sounds (show as pack) • oo oul u oo ue ew	**7. Write Sounds** • oo oul u oo ue ew
2. New Spelling: u-e Show the flashcard for **u-e**. Then with all the phonemes play the **Grab Game**. With the cards on the table, say a sound and ask the children to 'grab' for the letter. **Fingertips Freeze** when they touch the flashcard. Only allow one 'grab'.	**8. New Spelling: u-e** Model writing the letters on the board and talk through letter formations. **Sky Write** the letters together. Ask children to write the sound on their whiteboards or paper. Check the letter formations for the correct start points, exit strokes and place on the line.
3. Oral Blending (Robot Game) Play the **Robot Game**. Pretend to be a Robot who can only speak in sounds (robot speech), moving arms back and forth like robot arms, in time with each sound. • Say the sounds **L-(u-e)-k**, ask children to listen and say the word. • Repeat for: **prune, plume, flute**	**9. Oral Segmenting (Phoneme Fingers)** Say a word and the children use **Phoneme Fingers** to flick their fingers for each sound in: • **L-(u-e)-k, p-r-(u-e)-n, p-l-(u-e)-m, f-l-(u-e)-t**

4. Manipulating (Swap) Sounds

Stick vowel cards at the top of the board: **oo ue ew u-e**
Stick consonant cards at the bottom: **b d f l r t y**

Play the **Full Circle Word Game** using the letters on the board to make a word. Use two separate cards to make the split digraph u-e, ensuring children understand that this makes one sound. Ask the children to use **Phoneme Fingers** for each sound in the word. Read the word to the children. Ask a child to change one or more sounds in the word, swapping card/s from the word with card/s at either the bottom or the top of the board. Use **Phoneme Fingers** to make and read the new word. Continue the game changing one sound at a time until you get back to the first word made.

Full circle words: flew, flue, flute, loot, lute, brute, rude, rule, yule, fool, flew

5. Reading Words Ask children to read these words: • **Luke, prune, plume, flute**	**10. Word Dictation** Ask children to tap for the sounds and write: • **Luke, prune, plume, flute**
6. Reading Sentences (See page 129) Luke burnt the toast. Kay eats prunes with her cornflakes. A plume of smoke came from the tower. If Roy wins, it will be a fluke.	**11. Sentence Dictation** (See page 129) Luke burnt the toast. Kay eats prunes with her cornflakes. A plume of smoke came from the tower. If Roy wins, it will be a fluke. After writing, children read back sounds, words and sentences.

Snappy Lesson 60

STEP 3.1

Sound /oo/ written as ou

Learning Objectives: to learn the main ways of spelling the sound /oo/; to blend and segment words and sentences containing ou

Success Criteria: to read words and sentences containing ou spelling of sound /oo/ and write dictated words and sentences with 100% accuracy

Reading	Spelling
1. Review Sounds (show as pack) • oo oul u oo ue ew u-e	**7. Write Sounds** • oo oul u oo ue ew u-e
2. New Spelling: ou Show the flashcard for **ou**. Then with all the phonemes play the **Grab Game**. With the cards on the table, say a sound and ask the children to 'grab' for the letter. **Fingertips Freeze** when they touch the flashcard. Only allow one 'grab'.	**8. New Spelling: ou** Model writing the letters on the board and talk through letter formation from exit stroke of first letter to start point of the next letter for joined-up writing. **Sky Write** the letters together. Ask children to write the sound on their whiteboards or paper. Check the letter formation for the correct start points, exit strokes and place on the line.
3. Oral Blending (Robot Game) Play the **Robot Game**. Pretend to be a Robot who can only speak in sounds (robot speech), moving arms back and forth like robot arms, in time with each sound. • Say the sounds **y-ou**, ask children to listen and say the word. • Repeat for: **soup, group, coupon**	**9. Oral Segmenting (Phoneme Fingers)** Say a word and the children use **Phoneme Fingers** to flick their fingers for each sound in: • y-ou, s-ou-p, g-r-ou-p, c-ou-p-o-n

4. Manipulating (Swap) Sounds

Stick vowel cards at the top of the board: **oo ue ew u-e ou**
Stick consonant cards at the bottom: **c d f g l p r s y**

Play the **Full Circle Word Game** using the letters on the board to make a word. Use two separate cards to make the split digraph u-e, ensuring children understand that this makes one sound. Ask the children to use **Phoneme Fingers** for each sound in the word. Read the word to the children. Ask a child to change one or more sounds in the word, swapping card/s from the word with card/s at either the bottom or the top of the board. Use **Phoneme Fingers** to make and read the new word. Continue the game changing one sound at a time until you get back to the first word made.

Full circle words: you, yule, rule, rude, food, loop, soup, sue, screw, crew, clue, glue, group, you

5. Reading Words Ask children to read these words: • you, soup, group, coupon	**10. Word Dictation** Ask children to tap for the sounds and write: • you, soup, group, coupon
6. Reading Sentences (See page 129) Have you ever been to Africa? Steve will open a tin of soup. The group of children went out. Amy got free sweets with the coupon.	**11. Sentence Dictation** (See page 129) Have you ever been to Africa? Steve will open a tin of soup. The group of children went out. Amy got free sweets with the coupon. After writing, children read back sounds, words and sentences.

Snappy Lesson 61

STEP 3.1

Sound /oo/ written as o

Learning Objectives: to learn the main ways of spelling the sound /oo/; to blend and segment words and sentences containing o

Success Criteria: to read words and sentences containing o spelling of sound /oo/ and write dictated words and sentences with 100% accuracy

Reading	Spelling
1. Review Sounds (show as pack) • oo oul u oo ue ew u-e ou	**7. Write Sounds** • oo oul u oo ue ew u-e ou
2. New Spelling: o Show the flashcard for **o**. Then with all the phonemes play the **Grab Game**. With the cards on the table, say a sound and ask the children to 'grab' for the letter. **Fingertips Freeze** when they touch the flashcard. Only allow one 'grab'.	**8. New Spelling: o** Model writing the letter on the board and talk through letter formation. **Sky Write** the letter together. Ask children to write the sound on their whiteboards or paper. Check the letter formation for the correct start point, exit stroke and place on the line.
3. Oral Blending (Robot Game) Play the **Robot Game**. Pretend to be a Robot who can only speak in sounds (robot speech), moving arms back and forth like robot arms, in time with each sound. • Say the sounds **t-o**, ask children to listen and say the word. • Repeat for: **do, into, tonight**	**9. Oral Segmenting (Phoneme Fingers)** Say a word and the children use **Phoneme Fingers** to flick their fingers for each sound in: • t-o, d-o, i-n-t-o, t-o-n-igh-t

4. Manipulating (Swap) Sounds

Stick vowel cards at the top of the board: **oo ue ew u-e ou o**
Stick consonant cards at the bottom: **c d f g n p r s t**

Play the **Full Circle Word Game** using the letters on the board to make a word. Use two separate cards to make the split digraph u-e, ensuring children understand that this makes one sound. Ask the children to use **Phoneme Fingers** for each sound in the word. Read the word to the children. Ask a child to change one or more sounds in the word, swapping card/s from the word with card/s at either the bottom or the top of the board. Use **Phoneme Fingers** to make and read the new word. Continue the game changing one sound at a time until you get back to the first word made.

Full circle words: food, rude, true, to, do, drew, screw, group, soup, soon, food

5. Reading Words Ask children to read these words: • to, do, into, tonight	**10. Word Dictation** Ask children to tap for the sounds and write: • to, do, into, tonight
6. Reading Sentences (See page 130) They are flying to Canada by plane. Do the houses have outside lights? The boxes fit into the case. Can Pete come for supper tonight?	**11. Sentence Dictation** (See page 130) They are flying to Canada by plane. Do the houses have outside lights? The boxes fit into the case. Can Pete come for supper tonight? After writing, children read back sounds, words and sentences.

Snappy Lesson 62 *FastTrack*

STEP 3.1

Review: Sound /oo/ written as oo, ue, ew, u-e, ou, o

Learning Objectives: to review a set of letter/sound correspondences; to learn the main ways of spelling the sound /oo/, read these spelling choices in words and sentences and write them in dictated words and sentences.

Example grid:

oo	ue	ew	u-e	ou	o
too	clue	blew	June	you	do
zoo	blue	chew	flute	soup	to
boot	glue	grew	rude	group	into
food	true	drew	rule		today
soon	Sue	flew	brute		
spoon	tissue	screw	conclude		

1. Draw a blank six-column grid on the board and explain that the group will be finding the main ways that the sound /oo/ can be written down.

2. Show the flashcard for /oo/ and ask children the main ways of writing the /oo/ sound. They may use letter names. Write the graphemes at the top of the columns on the grid.

3. Ask the children to say a word that contains the sound /oo/ and then to say which column it goes into. Write the choice in the correct column.

4. Ask the children to continue to generate examples while you write them in the correct column. There are some examples shown in the grid above if the children need prompting. Keep going until the columns are full.

5. Ask one child to come to the board, read the words in that column, underline the pattern, and comment on the position of the alternative spelling pattern in the word (i.e. beginning, middle or end).

6. Ask children to come to the board in turn until all of the alternative spelling patterns have been read, underlined and the position of the alternative spelling pattern commented on.

7. Children copy the grid into their books. Explain that they can add to this over time. Alternatively, make copies of the grid (see page 130) and stick these into the children's books. Explain that the words in this grid may not be exactly the same as those the children came up with.

8. Remove the grid from the board and dictate words (see example grid above) and the following sentences to the group for them to write down on a clean page or mini-whiteboard.

    He will soon eat his food with a spoon.
    Sue needs glue to mend the blue dish.
    The artist drew the birds as they flew off.
    June plays the flute quite well.
    Do you want some soup?
    What do you want to do today?

9. After writing the dictation, ask the children to read back a selection of words and sentences. Check for correct spelling choices and punctuation.

10. Ask the children to write a sentence of their own, using one of the words they have encountered. Listen to the children say the sentences aloud first. Moderate grammar and check for correct spelling choices and punctuation.

Snappy Lesson 63

STEP 3.1

Sound /e/ written as e

Learning Objectives: to learn the main ways of spelling the sound /e/; to blend and segment words and sentences containing e

Success Criteria: to read words and sentences containing e spelling of sound /e/ and write dictated words and sentences with 100% accuracy

Reading	Spelling
1. Review Sounds (show as pack) • oo ue ew u-e ou o	**8. Write Sounds** • oo ue ew u-e ou o
2. Spelling: e Show the flashcard for **e**. Then with all the phonemes play the **Grab Game**. With the cards on the table, say a sound and ask the children to 'grab' for the letter. **Fingertips Freeze** when they touch the flashcard. Only allow one 'grab'.	**9. Spelling: e** Model writing the letter on the board and talk through letter formation. **Sky Write** the letter together. Ask children to write the sound on their whiteboards or paper. Check the letter formation for the correct start point, exit stroke and place on the line.
3. Oral Blending (Robot Game) Play the **Robot Game**. Pretend to be a Robot who can only speak in sounds (robot speech), moving arms back and forth like robot arms, in time with each sound. • Say the sounds **p-e-t**, ask children to listen and say the word. • Repeat for: **bed, men, shelf**	**10. Oral Segmenting (Phoneme Fingers)** Say a word and the children use **Phoneme Fingers** to flick their fingers for each sound in: • p-e-t, b-e-d, m-e-n, sh-e-l-f

4. Manipulating (Swap) Sounds

Stick vowel cards at the top of the board: **a e ai ee ie oa ue**. Stick consonant cards at the bottom: **b c d d t**

Play the **Full Circle Word Game** using the letters on the board to make a word. Ask the children to use **Phoneme Fingers** for each sound in the word. Read the word to the children. Ask a child to change one or more sounds in the word, swapping card/s from the word with card/s at either the bottom or the top of the board. Use **Phoneme Fingers** to make and read the new word. Continue the game changing one sound at a time until you get back to the first word made.

Full circle words: bed, bait, beet, boat, coat, cue, due, die, dad, bad, bed

5. Reading Words Ask children to read these words: • pet, bed, men, shelf	**11. Word Dictation** Ask children to tap for the sounds and write: • pet, bed, men, shelf
6. Reading Tricky Words: their • Show flashcard with the tricky bit underlined. • Together, with the children, sound and say the word using the known letter/sound matches. • Point out that the word doesn't sound like this, identify the tricky bit, and provide tricky sound: the 'eir' sounds /air/. • Sound and say the word correctly together.	**12. Tricky Words Dictation: th**eir • Say the tricky word and remind children to watch out for the tricky bit. • Ask children to say the word, tap for the sounds and write each grapheme. Model with **Phoneme Fingers**, if necessary.
7. Reading Sentences (See page 130) Bob has three pets at home. Did you go to bed late? The men took their bags. Sally put up a shelf.	**13. Sentence Dictation** (See page 130) Bob has three pets at home. Did you go to bed late? The men took their bags. Sally put up a shelf. After writing, children read back sounds, words and sentences.

Snappy Lesson 64

STEP 3.1

Sound /e/ written as ea

Learning Objectives: to learn the main ways of spelling the sound /e/; to blend and segment words and sentences containing ea

Success Criteria: to read words and sentences containing e spelling of sound /ea/ and write dictated words and sentences with 100% accuracy

Reading	Spelling
1. Review Sounds (show as pack) • oo ue ew u-e ou o e	**7. Write Sounds** • oo ue ew u-e ou o e
2. New Spelling: ea Show the flashcard for **ea**. Then with all the phonemes play the **Grab Game**. With the cards on the table, say a sound and ask the children to 'grab' for the letter. **Fingertips Freeze** when they touch the flashcard. Only allow one 'grab'.	**8. New Spelling: ea** Model writing the letters on the board and talk through letter formation from exit stroke of first letter to start point of the next letter for joined-up writing. **Sky Write** the letters together. Ask children to write the sound on their whiteboards or paper. Check the letter formation for the correct start points, exit strokes and place on the line.
3. Oral Blending (Robot Game) Play the **Robot Game**. Pretend to be a Robot who can only speak in sounds (robot speech), moving arms back and forth like robot arms, in time with each sound. • Say the sounds **b-r-ea-d**, ask children to listen and say the word. • Repeat for: **ahead, ready, breakfast**	**9. Oral Segmenting (Phoneme Fingers)** Say a word and the children use **Phoneme Fingers** to flick their fingers for each sound in: • b-r-ea-d, a-h-ea-d, r-ea-d-y, b-r-ea-k-f-a-s-t

4. Manipulating (Swap) Sounds

Stick vowel cards at the top of the board: **a e ea**. Stick consonant cards at the bottom: **b d d f h l r**

Play the **Full Circle Word Game** using the letters on the board to make a word. Ask the children to use **Phoneme Fingers** for each sound in the word. Read the word to the children. Ask a child to change one or more sounds in the word, swapping card/s from the word with card/s at either the bottom or the top of the board. Use **Phoneme Fingers** to make and read the new word. Continue the game changing one sound at a time until you get back to the first word made.

• Full circle words: **dad, dead, head, had, fad, fed, led, lead, bed, bread, read, dead, dad**

5. Reading Words Ask children to read these words: • **bread, ahead, ready, breakfast**	**10. Word Dictation** Ask children to tap for the sounds and write: • **bread, ahead, ready, breakfast**
6. Reading Sentences (See page 131) I like to toast my bread. Let us sail full speed ahead. The plane is ready for take-off. Stan had fried bacon for breakfast.	**11. Sentence Dictation** (See page 131) I like to toast my bread. Let us sail full speed ahead. The plane is ready for take-off. Stan had fried bacon for breakfast. After writing, children read back sounds, words and sentences.

Snappy Lesson 65

STEP 3.1

Sound /e/ written as ai

Learning Objectives: to learn the main ways of spelling the sound /e/; to blend and segment words and sentences containing ai

Success Criteria: to read words and sentences containing ai spelling of sound /e/ and write dictated words and sentences with 100% accuracy

Reading	Spelling
1. Review Sounds (show as pack) • oo ue ew u-e ou o e ea	**7. Write Sounds** • oo ue ew u-e ou o e ea
2. New Spelling: ai Show the flashcard for **ai**. Then with all the phonemes play the **Grab Game**. With the cards on the table, say a sound and ask the children to 'grab' for the letter. **Fingertips Freeze** when they touch the flashcard. Only allow one 'grab'.	**8. New Spelling: ai** Model writing the letters on the board and talk through letter formation from exit stroke of first letter to start point of the next letter for joined-up writing. **Sky Write** the letters together. Ask children to write the sound on their whiteboards or paper. Check the letter formation for the correct start points, exit strokes and place on the line.
3. Oral Blending (Robot Game) Play the **Robot Game**. Pretend to be a Robot who can only speak in sounds (robot speech), moving arms back and forth like robot arms, in time with each sound. • Say the sounds **s-ai-d**, ask children to listen and say the word. • Repeat for: **again, against, unsaid**	**9. Oral Segmenting (Phoneme Fingers)** Say a word and the children use **Phoneme Fingers** to flick their fingers for each sound in: • **s-ai-d, a-g-ai-n, a-g-ai-n-s-t, u-n-s-ai-d**

4. Manipulating (Swap) Sounds

Stick vowel cards at the top of the board: **a u e ea ai**
Stick consonant cards at the bottom: **b d g h n r s**

Play the **Full Circle Word Game** using the letters on the board to make a word. Ask the children to use **Phoneme Fingers** for each sound in the word. Read the word to the children. Ask a child to change one or more sounds in the word, swapping card/s from the word with card/s at either the bottom or the top of the board. Use **Phoneme Fingers** to make and read the new word. Continue the game changing one sound at a time until you get back to the first word made.

Full circle words: bed, read, said, sad, had, ahead, again, gun, bun, bud, bed

5. Reading Words Ask children to read these words: • **said, again, against, unsaid**	**10. Word Dictation** Ask children to tap for the sounds and write: • **said, again, against, unsaid**
6. Reading Sentences (See page 131) He said we had to pay. The car ran out of oil again. The desk stood against the wall. What you said can't be unsaid.	**11. Sentence Dictation** (See page 131) He said we had to pay. The car ran out of oil again. The desk stood against the wall. What you said can't be unsaid. After writing, children read back sounds, words and sentences.

Snappy Lesson 66

STEP 3.1

Sound /e/ written as ie

Learning Objectives: to learn the main ways of spelling the sound /e/; to blend and segment words and sentences containing ie

Success Criteria: to read words and sentences containing ie spelling of sound /e/ and write dictated words and sentences with 100% accuracy

Reading	Spelling
1. Review Sounds (show as pack) • oo ue ew u-e ou o e ea ai	**7. Write Sounds** • oo ue ew u-e ou o e ea ai
2. New Spelling: ie Show the flashcard for **ie**. Then with all the phonemes play the **Grab Game**. With the cards on the table, say a sound and ask the children to 'grab' for the letter. **Fingertips Freeze** when they touch the flashcard. Only allow one 'grab'.	**8. New Spelling: ie** Model writing the letters on the board and talk through letter formation from exit stroke of first letter to start point of the next letter for joined-up writing. **Sky Write** the letters together. Ask children to write the sound on their whiteboards or paper. Check the letter formation for the correct start points, exit strokes and place on the line.
3. Oral Blending (Robot Game) Play the **Robot Game**. Pretend to be a Robot who can only speak in sounds (robot speech), moving arms back and forth like robot arms, in time with each sound. • Say the sounds **f-r-ie-n-d**, ask children to listen and say the word. • Repeat for: **friendship, friendly, unfriendly**	**9. Oral Segmenting (Phoneme Fingers)** Say a word and the children use **Phoneme Fingers** to flick their fingers for each sound in: • f-r-ie-n-d, f-r-ie-n-d-sh-i-p, f-r-ie-n-d-l-y, u-n-f-r-ie-n-d-l-y

4. Manipulating (Swap) Sounds

Stick vowel cards at the top of the board: **a e ea ai ie**
Stick consonant cards at the bottom: **d f l n r s**

Play the **Full Circle Word Game** using the letters on the board to make a word. Ask the children to use **Phoneme Fingers** for each sound in the word. Read the word to the children. Ask a child to change one or more sounds in the word, swapping card/s from the word with card/s at either the bottom or the top of the board. Use **Phoneme Fingers** to make and read the new word. Continue the game changing one sound at a time until you get back to the first word made.

Full circle words: led, lead, sad, said, send, friend, fend, lend, led

5. Reading Words Ask children to read these words: • friend, friendship, friendly, unfriendly	**10. Word Dictation** Ask children to tap for the sounds and write: • friend, friendship, friendly, unfriendly
6. Reading Sentences (See page 131) My friend Molly has a yellow kite. They have a strong friendship. The new teacher seems friendly. Wild dogs are unfriendly.	**11. Sentence Dictation** (See page 131) My friend Molly has a yellow kite. They have a strong friendship. The new teacher seems friendly. Wild dogs are unfriendly. After writing, children read back sounds, words and sentences.

Snappy Lesson 67 — FastTrack

STEP 3.1

Review: Sound /e/ written as e, ea, ai, ie

Learning Objectives: to review a set of letter/sound correspondences; to learn the main ways of spelling the sound /e/, read these spelling choices in words and sentences and write them in dictated words and sentences.

Example grid:

e	ea	ai	ie
get	head	said	friend
bed	dead	again	friendship
men	deaf	against	unfriendly
then	ready	unsaid	
neck	bread		
spend	instead		

1. Draw a blank four-column grid on the board and explain that the group will be finding the main ways that the sound /e/ can be written down.

2. Show the flashcard for /e/ and ask children the main ways of writing the /e/ sound. They may use letter names. Write the graphemes at the top of the columns on the grid.

3. Ask the children to say a word that contains the sound /e/ and then to say which column it goes into. Write the choice in the correct column.

4. Ask the children to continue to generate examples while you write them in the correct column. There are some examples shown in the grid above if the children need prompting. Keep going until the columns are full.

5. Ask one child to come to the board, read the words in that column, underline the pattern, and comment on the position of the alternative spelling pattern in the word (i.e. beginning, middle or end).

6. Ask children to come to the board in turn until all of the alternative spelling patterns have been read, underlined and the position of the alternative spelling pattern commented on.

7. Children copy the grid into their books. Explain that they can add to this over time. Alternatively, make copies of the grid (see page 132) and stick these into the children's books. Explain that the words in this grid may not be exactly the same as those the children came up with.

8. Remove the grid from the board and dictate words (see example grid above) and the following sentences to the group for them to write down on a clean page or mini-whiteboard.

   Ben went to bed at ten.
   If you are ready, you can get the bread now, instead of later.
   Liz said I can go again today.
   I went to the park with my friend.

9. After writing the dictation, ask the children to read back a selection of words and sentences. Check for correct spelling choices and punctuation.

10. Ask the children to write a sentence of their own, using one of the words they have encountered. Listen to the children say the sentences aloud first. Moderate grammar and check for correct spelling choices and punctuation.

Snappy Lesson 68

STEP 3.1

Sound /u/ written as u

Learning Objectives: to learn the main ways of spelling the sound /u/; to blend and segment words and sentences containing u

Success Criteria: to read words and sentences containing u spelling of sound /u/ and write dictated words and sentences with 100% accuracy

Reading	Spelling
1. Review Sounds (show as pack) • e ea ai ie	**8. Write Sounds** • e ea ai ie
2. Spelling: u Show the flashcard for **u**. Then with all the phonemes play the **Grab Game**. With the cards on the table, say a sound and ask the children to 'grab' for the letter. **Fingertips Freeze** when they touch the flashcard. Only allow one 'grab'.	**9. Spelling: u** Model writing the letter on the board and talk through letter formation. **Sky Write** the letter together. Ask children to write the sound on their whiteboards or paper. Check the letter formation for the correct start point, exit stroke and place on the line.
3. Oral Blending (Robot Game) Play the **Robot Game**. Pretend to be a Robot who can only speak in sounds (robot speech), moving arms back and forth like robot arms, in time with each sound. • Say the sounds **b-u-n**, ask children to listen and say the word. • Repeat for: **up, lunch, under**	**10. Oral Segmenting (Phoneme Fingers)** Say a word and the children use **Phoneme Fingers** to flick their fingers for each sound in: • b-u-n, u-p, l-u-n-ch, u-n-d-er

4. Manipulating (Swap) Sounds

Stick vowel cards at the top of the board: **a i oa o u**
Stick consonant cards at the bottom: **b m r s t**

Play the **Full Circle Word Game** using the letters on the board to make a word. Ask the children to use **Phoneme Fingers** for each sound in the word. Read the word to the children. Ask a child to change one or more sounds in the word, swapping card/s from the word with card/s at either the bottom or the top of the board. Use **Phoneme Fingers** to make and read the new word. Continue the game changing one sound at a time until you get back to the first word made.

Full circle words: bus, but, bust, must, mast, mist, most, boast, roast, rust, bust, bus

5. Reading Words Ask children to read these words: • bun, up, lunch, under	**11. Word Dictation** Ask children to tap for the sounds and write: • bun, up, lunch, under
6. Reading Tricky Words: Mr, Mrs • Show flashcards. • Explain that Mr and Mrs are shortened forms (abbreviations) of Mister and Missus. • In 'Mister' the first and last letters are used to abbreviate the word. Explain that 'Mrs' is like 'Mr' with an added 's'. Point out the 's' sounds in 'Missus' to help children remember this. • Say the words correctly together.	**12. Tricky Words Dictation: Mr, Mrs** • Say the tricky words and remind children that Mr and Mrs are shortened forms (abbreviations) of the words Mister and Missus. • Ask children to say the words and write down the shortened forms.
7. Reading Sentences (See page 132) We have hot cross buns at Easter. The baby sat up in her pram. Do you go home for lunch? Mr and Mrs Smith found a coin under the tree.	**13. Sentence Dictation** (See page 132) We have hot cross buns at Easter. The baby sat up in her pram. Do you go home for lunch? Mr and Mrs Smith found a coin under the tree. After writing, children read back sounds, words and sentences.

Snappy Lesson 69

STEP 3.1

Sound /u/ written as ou

Learning Objectives: to learn the main ways of spelling the sound /u/; to blend and segment words and sentences containing ou

Success Criteria: to read words and sentences containing ou spelling of sound /u/ and write dictated words and sentences with 100% accuracy

Reading	Spelling
1. Review Sounds (show as pack) • e ea ai ie u	**7. Write Sounds** • e ea ai ie u
2. New Spelling: ou Show the flashcard for **ou**. Then with all the phonemes play the **Grab Game**. With the cards on the table, say a sound and ask the children to 'grab' for the letter. **Fingertips Freeze** when they touch the flashcard. Only allow one 'grab'.	**8. New Spelling: ou** Model writing the letters on the board and talk through letter formation from exit stroke of first letter to start point of the next letter for joined-up writing. **Sky Write** the letters together. Ask children to write the sound on their whiteboards or paper. Check the letter formation for the correct start points, exit strokes and place on the line.
3. Oral Blending (Robot Game) Play the **Robot Game**. Pretend to be a Robot who can only speak in sounds (robot speech), moving arms back and forth like robot arms, in time with each sound. • Say the sounds **y-ou-ng**, ask children to listen and say the word. • Repeat for: **touch, cousin, famous**	**9. Oral Segmenting (Phoneme Fingers)** Say a word and the children use **Phoneme Fingers** to flick their fingers for each sound in: • y-ou-ng, t-ou-ch, c-ou-s-i-n, f-a-m-ou-s

4. Manipulating (Swap) Sounds

Stick vowel cards at the top of the board: **a u ou**
Stick consonant cards at the bottom: **m s t ch ng y**

Play the **Full Circle Word Game** using the letters on the board to make a word. Ask the children to use **Phoneme Fingers** for each sound in the word. Read the word to the children. Ask a child to change one or more sounds in the word, swapping card/s from the word with card/s at either the bottom or the top of the board. Use **Phoneme Fingers** to make and read the new word. Continue the game changing one sound at a time until you get back to the first word made.

Full circle words: much, touch, tang, young, sung, such, much

5. Reading Words Ask children to read these words: • young, touch, cousin, famous	**10. Word Dictation** Ask children to tap for the sounds and write: • young, touch, cousin, famous
6. Reading Sentences (See page 132) Steve is too young to join the army. You can look but not touch. Her cousin's name is Jane. The president is famous.	**11. Sentence Dictation** (See page 132) Steve is too young to join the army. You can look but not touch. Her cousin's name is Jane. The president is famous. After writing, children read back sounds, words and sentences.

Snappy Lesson 70

STEP 3.1

Sound /u/ written as o-e

Learning Objectives: to learn the main ways of spelling the sound /u/; to blend and segment words and sentences containing o-e

Success Criteria: to read words and sentences containing o-e spelling of sound /u/ and write dictated words and sentences with 100% accuracy

Reading	Spelling
1. Review Sounds (show as pack) • e ea ai ie u ou	**7. Write Sounds** • e ea ai ie u ou
2. New Spelling: o-e Show the flashcard for **o-e**. Then with all the phonemes play the **Grab Game**. With the cards on the table, say a sound and ask the children to 'grab' for the letter. **Fingertips Freeze** when they touch the flashcard. Only allow one 'grab'.	**8. New Spelling: o-e** Model writing the letters on the board and talk through letter formations. **Sky Write** the letters together. Ask children to write the sound on their whiteboards or paper. Check the letter formations for the correct start points, exit strokes and place on the line.
3. Oral Blending (Robot Game) Play the **Robot Game**. Pretend to be a Robot who can only speak in sounds (robot speech), moving arms back and forth like robot arms, in time with each sound. • Say the sounds **d-(o-e)-n**, ask children to listen and say the word. • Repeat for: **some, come, love**	**9. Oral Segmenting (Phoneme Fingers)** Say a word and the children use **Phoneme Fingers** to flick their fingers for each sound in: • d-(o-e)-n, s-(o-e)-m, c-(o-e)-m, l-(o-e)-v

4. Manipulating (Swap) Sounds

Stick vowel cards at the top of the board: **i u ou o-e**
Stick consonant cards at the bottom: **c d g l m n n s t v sh ch**

Play the **Full Circle Word Game** using the letters on the board to make a word. Use two separate cards to make the split digraph o-e, ensuring children understand that this makes one sound. Ask the children to use **Phoneme Fingers** for each sound in the word. Read the word to the children. Ask a child to change one or more sounds in the word, swapping card/s from the word with card/s at either the bottom or the top of the board. Use **Phoneme Fingers** to make and read the new word. Continue the game changing one sound at a time until you get back to the first word made.

Full circle words: touch, such, some, come, love, shove, glove, none, done, dun, din, tin, touch

5. Reading Words Ask children to read these words: • **done, some, come, love**	**10. Word Dictation** Ask children to tap for the sounds and write: • **done, some, come, love**
6. Reading Sentences (See page 133) **What has Jack done to the bike?** **Would you like some cake?** **When can Sue come to visit me?** **I love to see tulips in bloom.**	**11. Sentence Dictation** (See page 133) **What has Jack done to the bike?** **Would you like some cake?** **When can Sue come to visit me?** **I love to see tulips in bloom.** After writing, children read back sounds, words and sentences.

Snappy Lesson 71

STEP 3.1

Sound /u/ written as o

Learning Objectives: to learn the main ways of spelling the sound /u/; to blend and segment words and sentences containing o

Success Criteria: to read words and sentences containing o spelling of sound /u/ and write dictated words and sentences with 100% accuracy

Reading	Spelling
1. Review Sounds (show as pack) • e ea ai ie u ou o-e	**7. Write Sounds** • e ea ai ie u ou o-e
2. New Spelling: o Show the flashcard for **o**. Then with all the phonemes play the **Grab Game**. With the cards on the table, say a sound and ask the children to 'grab' for the letter. **Fingertips Freeze** when they touch the flashcard. Only allow one 'grab'.	**8. New Spelling: o** Model writing the letter on the board and talk through letter formation. **Sky Write** the letter together. Ask children to write the sound on their whiteboards or paper. Check the letter formation for the correct start point, exit stroke and place on the line.
3. Oral Blending (Robot Game) Play the **Robot Game**. Pretend to be a Robot who can only speak in sounds (robot speech), moving arms back and forth like robot arms, in time with each sound. • Say the sounds **s-o-n**, ask children to listen and say the word. • Repeat for: **month, mother, brother**	**9. Oral Segmenting (Phoneme Fingers)** Say a word and the children use **Phoneme Fingers** to flick their fingers for each sound in: • **s-o-n, m-o-n-th, m-o-th-er, b-r-o-th-er**

4. Manipulating (Swap) Sounds

Stick vowel cards at the top of the board: **u ou o-e o**
Stick consonant cards at the bottom: **c d f m n r s t w y ng**

Play the **Full Circle Word Game** using the letters on the board to make a word. Use two separate cards to make the split digraph o-e, ensuring children understand that this makes one sound. Ask the children to use **Phoneme Fingers** for each sound in the word. Read the word to the children. Ask a child to change one or more sounds in the word, swapping card/s from the word with card/s at either the bottom or the top of the board. Use **Phoneme Fingers** to make and read the new word. Continue the game changing one sound at a time until you get back to the first word made.

Full circle words: fun, son, won, ton, front, runt, run, done, dung, young, yum, come, some, sun, fun

5. Reading Words Ask children to read these words: • **son, month, mother, brother**	**10. Word Dictation** Ask children to tap for the sounds and write: • **son, month, mother, brother**
6. Reading Sentences (See page 133) My son is a teacher. The month of March was windy. Her mother likes flowers. His brother looks like him.	**11. Sentence Dictation** (See page 133) My son is a teacher. The month of March was windy. Her mother likes flowers. His brother looks like him. After writing, children read back sounds, words and sentences.

Snappy Lesson 72 *FastTrack*

STEP 3.1

Review: Sound /u/ written as u, ou, o-e, o

Learning Objectives: to review a set of letter/sound correspondences; to learn the main ways of spelling the sound /u/, read these spelling choices in words and sentences and write them in dictated words and sentences.

Example grid:

u	ou	o-e	o
up	young	some	son
mum	cousin	come	front
run	touch	done	month
cup	country	love	mother
bus	famous	honey	brother
sunset	trouble	money	discover

1. Draw a blank four-column grid on the board and explain that the group will be finding the main ways that the sound /u/ can be written down.

2. Show the flashcard for /u/ and ask children the main ways of writing the /u/ sound. They may use letter names. Write the graphemes at the top of the columns on the grid.

3. Ask the children to say a word that contains the sound /u/ and then to say which column it goes into. Write the choice in the correct column.

4. Ask the children to continue to generate examples while you write them in the correct column. There are some examples shown in the grid above if the children need prompting. Keep going until the columns are full.

5. Ask one child to come to the board, read the words in that column, underline the pattern, and comment on the position of the alternative spelling pattern in the word (i.e. beginning, middle or end).

6. Ask children to come to the board in turn until all of the alternative spelling patterns have been read, underlined and the position of the alternative spelling pattern commented on.

7. Children copy the grid into their books. Explain that they can add to this over time. Alternatively, make copies of the grid (see page 133) and stick these into the children's books. Explain that the words in this grid may not be exactly the same as those the children came up with.

8. Remove the grid from the board and dictate words (see example grid above) and the following sentences to the group for them to write down on a clean page or mini-whiteboard.

   Ted had to run for the bus.
   Our young cousin was in trouble.
   She needs some money for the gloves.
   My mother, my brother and my son painted the front room.

9. After writing the dictation, ask the children to read back a selection of words and sentences. Check for correct spelling choices and punctuation.

10. Ask the children to write a sentence of their own, using one of the words they have encountered. Listen to the children say the sentences aloud first. Moderate grammar and check for correct spelling choices and punctuation.

Review: Snappy Lesson 73

STEP 3.2

Sound /c/ written as c

Learning Objectives: to learn the main ways of spelling the sound /c/; to blend and segment words and sentences containing c

Success Criteria: to read words and sentences containing c spelling of sound /c/ and write dictated words and sentences with 100% accuracy

Reading	Spelling
1. Review Sounds (show as pack) • i y	**7. Write Sounds** • i y
2. Spelling: c Show the flashcard for **c**. Then with all the phonemes play the **Grab Game**. With the cards on the table, say a sound and ask the children to 'grab' for the letter. **Fingertips Freeze** when they touch the flashcard. Only allow one 'grab'.	**8. Spelling: c** Model writing the letter on the board and talk through letter formation. **Sky Write** the letter together. Ask children to write the sound on their whiteboards or paper. Check the letter formation for the correct start point, exit stroke and place on the line.
3. Oral Blending (Robot Game) Play the **Robot Game**. Pretend to be a Robot who can only speak in sounds (robot speech), moving arms back and forth like robot arms, in time with each sound. • Say the sounds **c-a-n**, ask children to listen and say the word. • Repeat for: **coal, crash, picnic**	**9. Oral Segmenting (Phoneme Fingers)** Say a word and the children use **Phoneme Fingers** to flick their fingers for each sound in: • **c-a-n, c-oa-l, c-r-a-sh, p-i-c-n-i-c**

4. Manipulating (Swap) Sounds

Stick vowel card at the top of the board: **a**
Stick consonant cards at the bottom: **m p r s c**

Play the **Full Circle Word Game** using the letters on the board to make a word. Ask the children to use **Phoneme Fingers** for each sound in the word. Read the word to the children. Ask a child to change one or more sounds in the word, swapping card/s from the word with card/s at either the bottom or the top of the board. Use **Phoneme Fingers** to make and read the new word. Continue the game changing one sound at a time until you get back to the first word made.

Full circle words: cap, camp, cramp, scamp, scrap, cap

5. Reading Words Ask children to read these words: • **can, coal, crash, picnic**	**10. Word Dictation** Ask children to tap for the sounds and write: • **can, coal, crash, picnic**
6. Reading Sentences (See page 134) Can you meet me in town? The miners found coal in the mine. He was hurt in a train crash. We went for a picnic by the river.	**11. Sentence Dictation** (See page 134) Can you meet me in town? The miners found coal in the mine. He was hurt in a train crash. We went for a picnic by the river. After writing, children read back sounds, words and sentences.

Snappy Lesson 74

STEP 3.2

Sound /c/ written as k

Learning Objectives: to learn the main ways of spelling the sound /c/; to blend and segment words and sentences containing k

Success Criteria: to read words and sentences containing c spelling of sound /k/ and write dictated words and sentences with 100% accuracy

Reading	Spelling
1. Review Sounds (show as pack) • ai a-e ay ey a c	**7. Write Sounds** • ai a-e ay ey a c
2. New Spelling: k Show the flashcard for **k**. Then with all the phonemes play the **Grab Game**. With the cards on the table, say a sound and ask the children to 'grab' for the letter. **Fingertips Freeze** when they touch the flashcard. Only allow one 'grab'.	**8. New Spelling: k** Model writing the letter on the board and talk through letter formation. **Sky Write** the letter together. Ask children to write the sound on their whiteboards or paper. Check the letter formation for the correct start point, exit stroke and place on the line.
3. Oral Blending (Robot Game) Play the **Robot Game**. Pretend to be a Robot who can only speak in sounds (robot speech), moving arms back and forth like robot arms, in time with each sound. • Say the sounds **k-i-ng**, ask children to listen and say the word. • Repeat for: **silk, skin, desk**	**9. Oral Segmenting (Phoneme Fingers)** Say a word and the children use **Phoneme Fingers** to flick their fingers for each sound in: • **k-i-ng, s-i-l-k, s-k-i-n, d-e-s-k**

4. Manipulating (Swap) Sounds

Stick vowel cards at the top of the board: **a e i o u**
Stick consonant cards at the bottom: **d p t n s c k**

Play the **Full Circle Word Game** using the letters on the board to make a word. Ask the children to use **Phoneme Fingers** for each sound in the word. Read the word to the children. Ask a child to change one or more sounds in the word, swapping card/s from the word with card/s at either the bottom or the top of the board. Use **Phoneme Fingers** to make and read the new word. Continue the game changing one sound at a time until you get back to the first word made.

Full circle words: cod, kid, cad, cap, kip, kept, kit, cut, cat, can, scan, skin, kin, con, cod

5. Reading Words Ask children to read these words: • **king, silk, skin, desk**	**10. Word Dictation** Ask children to tap for the sounds and write: • **king, silk, skin, desk**
6. Reading Sentences (See page 134) **The king sat on his throne.** **Andrew put on his silk tie.** **Sue has a dry skin.** **Is her desk in the study?**	**11. Sentence Dictation** (See page 134) **The king sat on his throne.** **Andrew put on his silk tie.** **Sue has a dry skin.** **Is her desk in the study?** After writing, children read back sounds, words and sentences.

Snappy Lesson 75

STEP 3.2

Sound /c/ written as ck

Learning Objectives: to learn the main ways of spelling the sound /c/; to blend and segment words and sentences containing ck

Success Criteria: to read words and sentences containing ck spelling of sound /c/ and write dictated words and sentences with 100% accuracy

Reading	Spelling
1. Review Sounds (show as pack) • ee ea e e-e c k	**7. Write Sounds** • ee ea e e-e c k
2. New Spelling: ck Show the flashcard for **ck**. Then with all the phonemes play the **Grab Game**. With the cards on the table, say a sound and ask the children to 'grab' for the letter. **Fingertips Freeze** when they touch the flashcard. Only allow one 'grab'.	**8. New Spelling: ck** Model writing the letters on the board and talk through letter formation from exit stroke of first letter to start point of the next letter for joined-up writing. **Sky Write** the letters together. Ask children to write the sound on their whiteboards or paper. Check the letter formation for the correct start points, exit strokes and place on the line.
3. Oral Blending (Robot Game) Play the **Robot Game**. Pretend to be a Robot who can only speak in sounds (robot speech), moving arms back and forth like robot arms, in time with each sound. • Say the sounds **d-u-ck**, ask children to listen and say the word. • Repeat for: **neck, sick, rock**	**9. Oral Segmenting (Phoneme Fingers)** Say a word and the children use **Phoneme Fingers** to flick their fingers for each sound in: • **d-u-ck, n-e-ck, s-i-ck, r-o-ck**

4. Manipulating (Swap) Sounds

Stick vowel cards at the top of the board: **a e i o u**
Stick consonant cards at the bottom: **b d p r s t t c k ck**

Play the **Full Circle Word Game** using the letters on the board to make a word. Ask the children to use **Phoneme Fingers** for each sound in the word. Read the word to the children. Ask a child to change one or more sounds in the word, swapping card/s from the word with card/s at either the bottom or the top of the board. Use **Phoneme Fingers** to make and read the new word. Continue the game changing one sound at a time until you get back to the first word made.

Full circle words: sack, sick, suck, sock, dock, deck, peck, pick, tick, ticket, cricket, bucket, buck, but, cut, kit, sit, sat, sack

5. Reading Words Ask children to read these words: • duck, neck, sick, rock	**10. Word Dictation** Ask children to tap for the sounds and write: • duck, neck, sick, rock
6. Reading Sentences (See page 134) The duck laid five eggs. Mother's neck became red in the sun. Sweet things can make you sick. These boys like to play on the rock.	**11. Sentence Dictation** (See page 134) The duck laid five eggs. Mother's neck became red in the sun. Sweet things can make you sick. These boys like to play on the rock. After writing, children read back sounds, words and sentences.

Snappy Lesson 76

STEP 3.2

Sound /c/ written as ch

Learning Objectives: to learn the main ways of spelling the sound /c/; to blend and segment words and sentences containing ch

Success Criteria: to read words and sentences containing ch spelling of sound /c/ and write dictated words and sentences with 100% accuracy

Reading	Spelling
1. Review Sounds (show as pack) • ie i-e igh y i c k ck	**7. Write Sounds** • ie i-e igh y i c k ck
2. Spelling: ch Show the flashcard for **ch**. Then with all the phonemes play the **Grab Game**. With the cards on the table, say a sound and ask the children to 'grab' for the letter. **Fingertips Freeze** when they touch the flashcard. Only allow one 'grab'.	**8. Spelling: ch** Model writing the letters on the board and talk through letter formation from exit stroke of first letter to start point of the next letter for joined-up writing. **Sky Write** the letters together. Ask children to write the sound on their whiteboards or paper. Check the letter formation for the correct start points, exit strokes and place on the line.
3. Oral Blending (Robot Game) Play the **Robot Game**. Pretend to be a Robot who can only speak in sounds (robot speech), moving arms back and forth like robot arms, in time with each sound. • Say the sounds **s-ch-oo-l**, ask children to listen and say the word. • Repeat for: **chorus, technical, chemist**	**9. Oral Segmenting (Phoneme Fingers)** Say a word and the children use **Phoneme Fingers** to flick their fingers for each sound in: • **s-ch-oo-l, ch-or-u-s, t-e-ch-n-i-c-a-l, ch-e-m-i-s-t**

4. Manipulating (Swap) Sounds

Stick vowel cards at the top of the board: **a i u oo**
Stick consonant cards at the bottom: **l m r s c k ck ch**

Play the **Full Circle Word Game** using the letters on the board to make a word. Ask the children to use **Phoneme Fingers** for each sound in the word. Read the word to the children. Ask a child to change one or more sounds in the word, swapping card/s from the word with card/s at either the bottom or the top of the board. Use **Phoneme Fingers** to make and read the new word. Continue the game changing one sound at a time until you get back to the first word made.

Full circle words: chris, risk, cask, mask, musk, muck, luck, cluck, cool, school, chris

5. Reading Words Ask children to read these words: • **school, chorus, technical, chemist**	**10. Word Dictation** Ask children to tap for the sounds and write: • **school, chorus, technical, chemist**
6. Reading Sentences (See page 135) The school opens in the morning. They all sing the chorus. Can you explain the technical details? The chemist closes at night.	**11. Sentence Dictation** (See page 134) The school opens in the morning. They all sing the chorus. Can you explain the technical details? The chemist closes at night. After writing, children read back sounds, words and sentences.

Snappy Lesson 77 *FastTrack*

STEP 3.2

Review: Sound /c/ written as c, k, ck, ch

Learning Objectives: to review a set of letter/sound correspondences; to learn the main ways of spelling the sound /c/, read these spelling choices in words and sentences and write them in dictated words and sentences.

Example grid:

c	k	ck	ch
can	kid	kick	school
cot	king	sock	Christmas
clog	keep	sack	chemist
crust	milk	stuck	chronic
coal	skip	pocket	chemical
cling	soak	ticket	headache

1. Draw a blank four-column grid on the board and explain that the group will be finding the main ways that the sound /c/ can be written down.

2. Show the flashcard for /c/ and ask children the main ways of writing the /c/ sound. They may use letter names. Write the graphemes at the top of the columns on the grid.

3. Ask the children to say a word that contains the sound /c/ and then to say which column it goes into. Write the choice in the correct column.

4. Ask the children to continue to generate examples while you write them in the correct column. There are some examples shown in the grid above if the children need prompting. Keep going until the columns are full.

5. Ask one child to come to the board, read the words in that column, underline the pattern, and comment on the position of the alternative spelling pattern in the word (i.e. beginning, middle or end).

6. Ask children to come to the board in turn until all of the alternative spelling patterns have been read, underlined and the position of the alternative spelling pattern commented on.

7. Children copy the grid into their books. Explain that they can add to this over time. Alternatively, make copies of the grid (see page 135) and stick these into the children's books. Explain that the words in this grid may not be exactly the same as those the children came up with.

8. Remove the grid from the board and dictate words (see example grid above) and the following sentences to the group for them to write down on a clean page or mini-whiteboard.

    Mum can put Carl in the cot.
    Kevin likes to drink milk.
    My ticket got stuck in my pocket.
    I had a headache at school today.

9. After writing the dictation, ask the children to read back a selection of words and sentences. Check for correct spelling choices and punctuation.

10. Ask the children to write a sentence of their own, using one of the words they have encountered. Listen to the children say the sentences aloud first. Moderate grammar and check for correct spelling choices and punctuation.

Snappy Lesson 78

STEP 3.2

Sound /j/ written as j

Learning Objectives: to learn the main ways of spelling the sound /j/; to blend and segment words and sentences containing j

Success Criteria: to read words and sentences containing j spelling of sound /j/ and write dictated words and sentences with 100% accuracy

Reading

1. Review Sounds (show as pack)
- oa o-e o ow c k ck ch

2. Spelling: j
Show the flashcard for **j**. Then with all the phonemes play the **Grab Game**. With the cards on the table, say a sound and ask the children to 'grab' for the letter. **Fingertips Freeze** when they touch the flashcard. Only allow one 'grab'.

3. Oral Blending (Robot Game)
Play the **Robot Game**. Pretend to be a Robot who can only speak in sounds (robot speech), moving arms back and forth like robot arms, in time with each sound.
- Say the sounds **j-o-b**, ask children to listen and say the word.
- Repeat for: **jam, jail, enjoy**

4. Manipulating (Swap) Sounds

Stick vowel cards at the top of the board: **a i o u ai oi**. Stick consonant cards at the bottom: **b g l m n j p**

Play the **Full Circle Word Game** using the letters on the board to make a word. Ask the children to use **Phoneme Fingers** for each sound in the word. Read the word to the children. Ask a child to change one or more sounds in the word, swapping card/s from the word with card/s at either the bottom or the top of the board. Use **Phoneme Fingers** to make and read the new word. Continue the game changing one sound at a time until you get back to the first word made.

Full circle words: jig, jog, jug, job, jab, jam, join, jail, pail, pain, pin, pig, jig

5. Reading Words
Ask children to read these words:
- **job, jam, jail, enjoy**

6. Reading Tricky Words: little
- Show flashcard with the tricky bit underlined.
- Together, with the children, sound and say the word using the known letter/sound matches.
- Point out that the word doesn't sound like this, identify the tricky bit, and provide tricky sound: the 'le' sounds /l/.
- Sound and say the word correctly together.

7. Reading Sentences (See page 135)

Prue lost her job at the bakers.
Did you finish the apricot jam?
The jail is now full.
Did you enjoy it a little?

Spelling

8. Write Sounds
- oa o-e o ow c k ck ch

9. Spelling: j
Model writing the letter on the board and talk through letter formation. **Sky Write** the letter together. Ask children to write the sound on their whiteboards or paper. Check the letter formation for the correct start point, exit stroke and place on the line.

10. Oral Segmenting (Phoneme Fingers)
Say a word and the children use **Phoneme Fingers** to flick their fingers for each sound in:
- **j-o-b, j-a-m, j-ai-l, e-n-j-oy**

11. Word Dictation
Ask children to tap for the sounds and write:
- **job, jam, jail, enjoy**

12. Tricky Words Dictation: little
- Say the tricky word and remind children to watch out for the tricky bit.
- Ask children to say the word, tap for the sounds and write each grapheme. Model with **Phoneme Fingers**, if necessary.

13. Sentence Dictation (See page 135)

Prue lost her job at the bakers.
Did you finish the apricot jam?
The jail is now full.
Did you enjoy it a little?

After writing, children read back sounds, words and sentences.

Snappy Lesson 79

STEP 3.2

Sound /j/ written as g(e) Letter g sounds /j/ when followed by the letter e

Learning Objectives: to learn the main ways of spelling the sound /j/; to blend and segment words and sentences containing g(e)

Success Criteria: to read words and sentences containing g(e) spelling of sound /j/ and write dictated words and sentences with 100% accuracy

Reading	Spelling
1. Review Sounds (show as pack) • ue u-e u ew c k ck ch j	**7. Write Sounds** • ue u-e u ew c k ck ch j
2. New Spelling: g(e) Show the flashcard for **g(e)**. Then with all the phonemes play the **Grab Game**. With the cards on the table, say a sound and ask the children to 'grab' for the letter. **Fingertips Freeze** when they touch the flashcard. Only allow one 'grab'.	**8. New Spelling: g(e)** Model writing the letters on the board and talk through letter formation from exit stroke of first letter to start point of the next letter for joined-up writing. **Sky Write** the letters together. Ask children to write the sound on their whiteboards or paper. Check the letter formation for the correct start points, exit strokes and place on the line.
3. Oral Blending (Robot Game) Play the **Robot Game**. Pretend to be a Robot who can only speak in sounds (robot speech), moving arms back and forth like robot arms, in time with each sound. • Say the sounds **g-e-m**, ask children to listen and say the word. • Repeat for: **gel, gerbil, generate**	**9. Oral Segmenting (Phoneme Fingers)** Say a word and the children use **Phoneme Fingers** to flick their fingers for each sound in: • g-e-m, g-e-l, g-er-b-i-l, g-e-n-er-(a-e)-t

4. Manipulating (Swap) Sounds

Stick vowel cards at the top of the board: **a e er**
Stick consonant cards at the bottom: **d l m n t ng j g**

Play the **Full Circle Word Game** using the letters on the board to make a word. Ask the children to use **Phoneme Fingers** for each sound in the word. Read the word to the children. Ask a child to change one or more sounds in the word, swapping card/s from the word with card/s at either the bottom or the top of the board. Use **Phoneme Fingers** to make and read the new word. Continue the game changing one sound at a time until you get back to the first word made.

Full circle words: jam, gem, gel, get, gent, agent, gender, gander, gang, jam

5. Reading Words Ask children to read these words: • **gem, gel, gerbil, generate**	**10. Word Dictation** Ask children to tap for the sounds and write: • **gem, gel, gerbil, generate**
6. Reading Sentences (See page 136) You are a gem. The gel came out of a tube. My pet gerbil was in a box. Hot coals generate heat.	**11. Sentence Dictation** (See page 136) You are a gem. The gel came out of a tube. My pet gerbil was in a box. Hot coals generate heat. After writing, children read back sounds, words and sentences.

Snappy Lesson 80

STEP 3.2

Sound /j/ written as g(i) Letter g sounds /j/ when followed by the letter i

Learning Objectives: to learn the main ways of spelling the sound /j/; to blend and segment words and sentences containing g(i)

Success Criteria: to read words and sentences containing g(i) spelling of sound /j/ and write dictated words and sentences with 100% accuracy

Reading

1. Review Sounds (show as pack)
- a ar c k ck ch j g(e)

2. New Spelling: g(i)
Show the flashcard for **g(i)**. Then with all the phonemes play the **Grab Game**. With the cards on the table, say a sound and ask the children to 'grab' for the letter. **Fingertips Freeze** when they touch the flashcard. Only allow one 'grab'.

3. Oral Blending (Robot Game)
Play the **Robot Game**. Pretend to be a Robot who can only speak in sounds (robot speech), moving arms back and forth like robot arms, in time with each sound.
- Say the sounds **m-a-g-i-c**, ask children to listen and say the word.
- Repeat for: **giant, ginger, margin**

Spelling

7. Write Sounds
- a ar c k ck ch j g(e)

8. New Spelling: g(i)
Model writing the letters on the board and talk through letter formation from exit stroke of first letter to start point of the next letter for joined-up writing. **Sky Write** the letters together. Ask children to write the sound on their whiteboards or paper. Check the letter formation for the correct start points, exit strokes and place on the line.

9. Oral Segmenting (Phoneme Fingers)
Say a word and the children use **Phoneme Fingers** to flick their fingers for each sound in:
- m-a-g-i-c, g-i-a-n-t, g-i-n-g-er, m-ar-g-i-n

4. Manipulating (Swap) Sounds

Stick vowel cards at the top of the board: **a e i o u**
Stick consonant cards at the bottom: **b m n j t g**

Play the **Full Circle Word Game** using the letters on the board to make a word. Ask the children to use **Phoneme Fingers** for each sound in the word. Read the word to the children. Ask a child to change one or more sounds in the word, swapping card/s from the word with card/s at either the bottom or the top of the board. Use **Phoneme Fingers** to make and read the new word. Continue the game changing one sound at a time until you get back to the first word made.

Full circle words: jam, gem, gin, gun, gut, jut, job, jog, jug, jag, jam

5. Reading Words
Ask children to read these words:
- magic, giant, ginger, margin

10. Word Dictation
Ask children to tap for the sounds and write:
- magic, giant, ginger, margin

6. Reading Sentences (See page 136)
Jack has a box of magic tricks.
Kate read a story about a giant.
Have you seen Patrick's ginger cat?
I will draw a margin on the paper.

11. Sentence Dictation (See page 136)
Jack has a box of magic tricks.
Kate read a story about a giant.
Have you seen Patrick's ginger cat?
I will draw a margin on the paper.

After writing, children read back sounds, words and sentences.

Snappy Lesson 81

STEP 3.2

Sound /j/ written as g(y) Letter g sounds /j/ when followed by the letter y

Learning Objectives: to learn the main ways of spelling the sound /j/; to blend and segment words and sentences containing g(y)

Success Criteria: to read words and sentences containing g(y) spelling of sound /j/ and write dictated words and sentences with 100% accuracy

Reading	Spelling
1. Review Sounds (show as pack) • er ur ir c k ck ch j g(e) g(i)	**7. Write Sounds** • er ur ir c k ck ch j g(e) g(i)
2. New Spelling: g(y) Show the flashcard for **g(y)**. Then with all the phonemes play the **Grab Game**. With the cards on the table, say a sound and ask the children to 'grab' for the letter. **Fingertips Freeze** when they touch the flashcard. Only allow one 'grab'.	**8. New Spelling: g(y)** Model writing the letters on the board and talk through letter formations. **Sky Write** the letters together. Ask children to write the sound on their whiteboards or paper. Check the letter formations for the correct start points, exit strokes and place on the line.
3. Oral Blending (Robot Game) Play the **Robot Game**. Pretend to be a Robot who can only speak in sounds (robot speech), moving arms back and forth like robot arms, in time with each sound. • Say the sounds **g-y-m**, ask children to listen and say the word. • Repeat for: **energy, Egypt, gypsy**	**9. Oral Segmenting (Phoneme Fingers)** Say a word and the children use **Phoneme Fingers** to flick their fingers for each sound in: • g-y-m, e-n-er-g-y, E-g-y-p-t, g-y-p-s-y

4. Manipulating (Swap) Sounds

Stick vowel cards at the top of the board: **a e i o u y y**
Stick consonant cards at the bottom: **m n p s t j g**

Play the **Full Circle Word Game** using the letters on the board to make a word. Ask the children to use **Phoneme Fingers** for each sound in the word. Read the word to the children. Ask a child to change one or more sounds in the word, swapping card/s from the word with card/s at either the bottom or the top of the board. Use **Phoneme Fingers** to make and read the new word. Continue the game changing one sound at a time until you get back to the first word made.

Full circle words: jog, jag, jam, gym, gem, gin, gun, gap, gyp, egypt, gypsy, tipsy, tip, top, tog, jog

5. Reading Words Ask children to read these words: • gym, energy, Egypt, gypsy	**10. Word Dictation** Ask children to tap for the sounds and write: • gym, energy, Egypt, gypsy
6. Reading Sentences (See page 136) Gym club meets after school. The puppy has too much energy. They went to Egypt on holiday. The gypsy caravan is painted yellow.	**11. Sentence Dictation** (See page 136) Gym club meets after school. The puppy has too much energy. They went to Egypt on holiday. The gypsy caravan is painted yellow. After writing, children read back sounds, words and sentences.

Snappy Lesson 82

STEP 3.2

Sound /j/ written as ge

Learning Objectives: to learn the main ways of spelling the sound /j/; to blend and segment words and sentences containing ge

Success Criteria: to read words and sentences containing ge spelling of sound /j/ and write dictated words and sentences with 100% accuracy

Reading	Spelling
1. Review Sounds (show as pack) • or au aw al c k ck ch j g(e) g(i) g(y)	**7. Write Sounds** • or au aw al c k ck ch j g(e) g(i) g(y)
2. New Spelling: ge Show the flashcard for **ge**. Then with all the phonemes play the **Grab Game**. With the cards on the table, say a sound and ask the children to 'grab' for the letter. **Fingertips Freeze** when they touch the flashcard. Only allow one 'grab'.	**8. New Spelling: ge** Model writing the letters on the board and talk through letter formation from exit stroke of first letter to start point of the next letter for joined-up writing. **Sky Write** the letters together. Ask children to write the sound on their whiteboards or paper. Check the letter formation for the correct start points, exit strokes and place on the line.
3. Oral Blending (Robot Game) Play the **Robot Game**. Pretend to be a Robot who can only speak in sounds (robot speech), moving arms back and forth like robot arms, in time with each sound. • Say the sounds **Ge-or-ge**, ask children to listen and say the word. • Repeat for: **barge, college, gorge**	**9. Oral Segmenting (Phoneme Fingers)** Say a word and the children use **Phoneme Fingers** to flick their fingers for each sound in: • **Ge-or-ge, b-ar-ge, c-o-ll-e-ge, g-or-ge**

4. Manipulating (Swap) Sounds

Stick vowel cards at the top of the board: **a i u er or y ou**
Stick consonant cards at the bottom: **f m n s j g g ge ge**

Play the **Full Circle Word Game** using the letters on the board to make a word. Ask the children to use **Phoneme Fingers** for each sound in the word. Read the word to the children. Ask a child to change one or more sounds in the word, swapping card/s from the word with card/s at either the bottom or the top of the board. Use **Phoneme Fingers** to make and read the new word. Continue the game changing one sound at a time until you get back to the first word made.

Full circle words: gorge, george, forge, for, form, jam, gym, gin, ginger, gun, gas, gorgeous, gorge

5. Reading Words Ask children to read these words: • **George, barge, college, gorge**	**10. Word Dictation** Ask children to tap for the sounds and write: • **George, barge, college, gorge**
6. Reading Sentences (See page 137) My brother's name is George. Coal was transported by barge. Nathan has gone to college. The Avon Gorge is in Bristol.	**11. Sentence Dictation** (See page 137) My brother's name is George. Coal was transported by barge. Nathan has gone to college. The Avon Gorge is in Bristol. After writing, children read back sounds, words and sentences.

Snappy Lesson 83

STEP 3.2

Sound /j/ written as dge

Learning Objectives: to learn the main ways of spelling the sound /j/; to blend and segment words and sentences containing dge

Success Criteria: to read words and sentences containing dge spelling of sound /j/ and write dictated words and sentences with 100% accuracy

Reading	Spelling
1. Review Sounds (show as pack) • oi oy c k ck ch j g(e) g(i) g(y) ge	**7. Write Sounds** • oi oy c k ck ch j g(e) g(i) g(y) ge
2. New Spelling: dge Show the flashcard for **dge**. Then with all the phonemes play the **Grab Game**. With the cards on the table, say a sound and ask the children to 'grab' for the letter. **Fingertips Freeze** when they touch the flashcard. Only allow one 'grab'.	**8. New Spelling: dge** Model writing the letters on the board and talk through letter formation from exit stroke of first letter to start point of the next letter for joined-up writing. **Sky Write** the letters together. Ask children to write the sound on their whiteboards or paper. Check the letter formation for the correct start points, exit strokes and place on the line.
3. Oral Blending (Robot Game) Play the **Robot Game**. Pretend to be a Robot who can only speak in sounds (robot speech), moving arms back and forth like robot arms, in time with each sound. • Say the sounds **b-r-i-dge**, ask children to listen and say the word. • Repeat for: **badge, nudge, hedge**	**9. Oral Segmenting (Phoneme Fingers)** Say a word and the children use **Phoneme Fingers** to flick their fingers for each sound in: • **b-r-i-dge, b-a-dge, n-u-dge, h-e-dge**

4. Manipulating (Swap) Sounds

Stick vowel cards at the top of the board: **a e i u ar y**
Stick consonant cards at the bottom: **b d f h l m n t j g ge dge**

Play the **Full Circle Word Game** using the letters on the board to make a word. Ask the children to use **Phoneme Fingers** for each sound in the word. Read the word to the children. Ask a child to change one or more sounds in the word, swapping card/s from the word with card/s at either the bottom or the top of the board. Use **Phoneme Fingers** to make and read the new word. Continue the game changing one sound at a time until you get back to the first word made.

Full circle words: bad, badge, ledge, edge, hedge, fudge, fun, gun, gin, gent, gem, gym, jam, jar, barge, bar, bad

5. Reading Words Ask children to read these words: • bridge, badge, nudge, hedge	**10. Word Dictation** Ask children to tap for the sounds and write: • bridge, badge, nudge, hedge
6. Reading Sentences (See page 137) The bridge goes over the river. He has a badge on his uniform. Can Judith give Dylan a nudge? The gardener cut the hedge.	**11. Sentence Dictation** (See page 137) The bridge goes over the river. He has a badge on his uniform. Can Judith give Dylan a nudge? The gardener cut the hedge. After writing, children read back sounds, words and sentences.

Snappy Lesson 84 *FastTrack*

STEP 3.2

Review: Sound /j/ written as j, g(e), g(i), g(y), ge, dge

Learning Objectives: to review a set of letter/sound correspondences; to learn the main ways of spelling the sound /j/, read these spelling choices in words and sentences and write them in dictated words and sentences.

Example grid:

j	g(e)	g(i)	g(y)	ge	dge
jam	gel	gin	gym	age	fudge
jet	gem	magic	gymnast	page	hedge
jig	gent	ginger	gypsy	sausage	ridge
jog	agent	giraffe	Egypt	George	ledge
join	gently	giblets	energy	barge	badge
jacket	danger	giant	synergy	college	badger

1. Draw a blank six-column grid on the board and explain that the group will be finding the main ways that the sound /j/ can be written down.

2. Show the flashcard for /j/ and ask children the main ways of writing the /j/ sound. They may use letter names. Write the graphemes at the top of the columns on the grid.

3. Ask the children to say a word that contains the sound /j/ and then to say which column it goes into. Write the choice in the correct column.

4. Ask the children to continue to generate examples while you write them in the correct column. There are some examples shown in the grid above if the children need prompting. Keep going until the columns are full.

5. Ask one child to come to the board, read the words in that column, underline the pattern, and comment on the position of the alternative spelling pattern in the word (i.e. beginning, middle or end).

6. Ask children to come to the board in turn until all of the alternative spelling patterns have been read, underlined and the position of the alternative spelling pattern commented on.

7. Children copy the grid into their books. Explain that they can add to this over time. Alternatively, make copies of the grid (see page 137) and stick these into the children's books. Explain that the words in this grid may not be exactly the same as those the children came up with.

8. Remove the grid from the board and dictate words (see example grid above) and the following sentences to the group for them to write down on a clean page or mini-whiteboard.

   The jumbo jet flew to Japan.
   This gem stone is a ruby.
   Jack had some magic beans and met a giant in this book.
   We will need a lot of energy at the gym club.
   George turned the page over.
   His house is on top of the ridge, behind a tall hedge.

9. After writing the dictation, ask the children to read back a selection of words and sentences. Check for correct spelling choices and punctuation.

10. Ask the children to write a sentence of their own, using one of the words they have encountered. Listen to the children say the sentences aloud first. Moderate grammar and check for correct spelling choices and punctuation.

Snappy Lesson 85

STEP 3.2

Sound /ch/ written as ch

Learning Objectives: learn the main ways of spelling the sound /ch/; to blend and segment words and sentences containing ch

Success Criteria: to read words and sentences containing ch spelling of sound /ch/ and write dictated words and sentences with 100% accuracy

Reading	Spelling
1. Review Sounds (show as pack) • ou ow j g(e) g(i) g(y) ge dge	**8. Write Sounds** • ou ow j g(e) g(i) g(y) ge dge
2. Spelling: ch Show the flashcard for **ch**. Then with all the phonemes play the **Grab Game**. With the cards on the table, say a sound and ask the children to 'grab' for the letter. **Fingertips Freeze** when they touch the flashcard. Only allow one 'grab'.	**9. Spelling: ch** Model writing the letters on the board and talk through letter formation from exit stroke of first letter to start point of the next letter for joined-up writing. **Sky Write** the letters together. Ask children to write the sound on their whiteboards or paper. Check the letter formation for the correct start points, exit strokes and place on the line.
3. Oral Blending (Robot Game) Play the **Robot Game**. Pretend to be a Robot who can only speak in sounds (robot speech), moving arms back and forth like robot arms, in time with each sound. • Say the sounds **ch-i-p-s**, ask children to listen and say the word. • Repeat for: **lunch, coach, chicken**	**10. Oral Segmenting (Phoneme Fingers)** Say a word and the children use **Phoneme Fingers** to flick their fingers for each sound in: • **ch-i-p-s, l-u-n-ch, c-oa-ch, ch-i-ck-e-n**
4. Manipulating (Swap) Sounds Stick vowel cards at the top of the board: **i o u**. Stick consonant cards at the bottom: **c h m n p r s ch** Play the **Full Circle Word Game** using the letters on the board to make a word. Ask the children to use **Phoneme Fingers** for each sound in the word. Read the word to the children. Ask a child to change one or more sounds in the word, swapping card/s from the word with card/s at either the bottom or the top of the board. Use **Phoneme Fingers** to make and read the new word. Continue the game changing one sound at a time until you get back to the first word made. **Full circle words: cops, chops, hops, hips, chips, much, such, rich, chin, chip, chop, cop, cops**	
5. Reading Words Ask children to read these words: • **chips, lunch, coach, chicken**	**11. Word Dictation** Ask children to tap for the sounds and write: • **chips, lunch, coach, chicken**
6. Reading Tricky Words: water • Show flashcard with the tricky bit underlined. • Together, with the children, sound and say the word using the known letter/sound matches. • Point out that the word doesn't sound like this, identify the tricky bit, and provide tricky sound: the 'a' sounds /or/. • Sound and say the word correctly together.	**12. Tricky Words Dictation: water** • Say the tricky word and remind children to watch out for the tricky bit. • Ask children to say the word, tap for the sounds and write each grapheme. Model with **Phoneme Fingers**, if necessary.
7. Reading Sentences (See page 138) I want fish and chips for tea. We have lunch at one o'clock. They took the coach to London. The chicken must have some water.	**13. Sentence Dictation** (See page 138) I want fish and chips for tea. We have lunch at one o'clock. They took the coach to London. The chicken must have some water. After writing, children read back sounds, words and sentences.

Snappy Lesson 86

STEP 3.2

Sound /ch/ written as tch

Learning Objectives: learn the main ways of spelling the sound /ch/; to blend and segment words and sentences containing tch

Success Criteria: read to read words and sentences containing tch spelling of sound /ch/ and write dictated words and sentences with 100% accuracy

Reading

1. Review Sounds (show as pack)
- oo oul u j g(e) g(i) g(y) ge dge ch

2. New Spelling: tch

Show the flashcard for **tch**. Then with all the phonemes play the **Grab Game**. With the cards on the table, say a sound and ask the children to 'grab' for the letter. **Fingertips Freeze** when they touch the flashcard. Only allow one 'grab'.

3. Oral Blending (Robot Game)

Play the **Robot Game**. Pretend to be a Robot who can only speak in sounds (robot speech), moving arms back and forth like robot arms, in time with each sound.

- Say the sounds **d-i-tch**, ask children to listen and say the word.
- Repeat for: **ditch, scratch, match, latch**

4. Manipulating (Swap) Sounds

Stick vowel cards at the top of the board: **a e i u**
Stick consonant cards at the bottom: **b c f h m n p s t th ch tch**

Play the **Full Circle Word Game** using the letters on the board to make a word. Ask the children to use **Phoneme Fingers** for each sound in the word. Read the word to the children. Ask a child to change one or more sounds in the word, swapping card/s from the word with card/s at either the bottom or the top of the board. Use **Phoneme Fingers** to make and read the new word. Continue the game changing one sound at a time until you get back to the first word made.

Full circle words: that, thatch, hatch, catch, fetch, pitch, itch, hitch, hutch, much, such, sun, bun, ban, bat, that

5. Reading Words

Ask children to read these words:
- **ditch, scratch, match, latch**

6. Reading Sentences (See page 138)

Chris rode his bike into a ditch.
Did the cat scratch your hand?
The football match is on Saturday.
The garden gate has a latch.

Spelling

7. Write Sounds
- oo oul u j g(e) g(i) g(y) ge dge ch

8. New Spelling: tch

Model writing the letters on the board and talk through letter formation from exit stroke of first letter to start point of the next letter for joined-up writing. **Sky Write** the letters together. Ask children to write the sound on their whiteboards or paper. Check the letter formation for the correct start points, exit strokes and place on the line.

9. Oral Segmenting (Phoneme Fingers)

Say a word and the children use **Phoneme Fingers** to flick their fingers for each sound in:
- **d-i-tch, s-c-r-a-tch, m-a-tch, l-a-tch**

10. Word Dictation

Ask children to tap for the sounds and write:
- **ditch, scratch, match, latch**

11. Sentence Dictation (See page 138)

Chris rode his bike into a ditch.
Did the cat scratch your hand?
The football match is on Saturday.
The garden gate has a latch.

After writing, children read back sounds, words and sentences.

Snappy Lesson 87 *FastTrack*

STEP 3.2

Review: Sound /ch/ written as ch, tch

Learning Objectives: to review a set of letter/sound correspondences; to learn the main ways of spelling the sound /ch/, read these spelling choices in words and sentences and write them in dictated words and sentences.

Example grid:

ch	tch
chop	catch
chin	fetch
chug	notch
check	stitch
such	match
March	kitchen

1. Draw a blank two-column grid on the board and explain that the group will be finding the main ways that the sound /ch/ can be written down.

2. Show the flashcard for /ch/ and ask children the main ways of writing the /ch/ sound. They may use letter names. Write the graphemes at the top of the columns on the grid.

3. Ask the children to say a word that contains the sound /ch/ and then to say which column it goes into. Write the choice in the correct column.

4. Ask the children to continue to generate examples while you write them in the correct column. There are some examples shown in the grid above if the children need prompting. Keep going until the columns are full.

5. Ask one child to come to the board, read the words in that column, underline the pattern, and comment on the position of the alternative spelling pattern in the word (i.e. beginning, middle or end).

6. Ask children to come to the board in turn until all of the alternative spelling patterns have been read, underlined and the position of the alternative spelling pattern commented on.

7. Children copy the grid into their books. Explain that they can add to this over time. Alternatively, make copies of the grid (see page 138) and stick these into the children's books. Explain that the words in this grid may not be exactly the same as those the children came up with.

8. Remove the grid from the board and dictate words (see example grid above) and the following sentences to the group for them to write down on a clean page or mini-whiteboard.

    I will check if we can have chips for lunch.
    Dad went to fetch a match from the kitchen.

9. After writing the dictation, ask the children to read back a selection of words and sentences. Check for correct spelling choices and punctuation.

10. Ask the children to write a sentence of their own, using one of the words they have encountered. Listen to the children say the sentences aloud first. Moderate grammar and check for correct spelling choices and punctuation.

Snappy Lesson 88

STEP 3.2

Sounds /ng+k/ written as nk

Learning Objectives: to learn the main way of spelling the sounds /ng+k/; to blend and segment words and sentences containing nk

Success Criteria: to read words and sentences containing nk spelling of sound /ng+k/ and write dictated words and sentences with 100% accuracy

Reading	Spelling
1. Review Sounds (show as pack) • oo ue ew u-e ou o ch tch	**8. Write Sounds** • oo ue ew u-e ou o ch tch
2. New Spelling: nk Show the flashcard for **nk**. Then with all the phonemes play the **Grab Game**. With the cards on the table, say a sound and ask the children to 'grab' for the letter. **Fingertips Freeze** when they touch the flashcard. Only allow one 'grab'.	**9. New Spelling: nk** Model writing the letters on the board and talk through letter formation from exit stroke of first letter to start point of the next letter for joined-up writing. **Sky Write** the letters together. Ask children to write the sound on their whiteboards or paper. Check the letter formation for the correct start points, exit strokes and place on the line.
3. Oral Blending (Robot Game) Play the **Robot Game**. Pretend to be a Robot who can only speak in sounds (robot speech), moving arms back and forth like robot arms, in time with each sound. • Say the sounds **p-i-n-k**, ask children to listen and say the word. • Repeat for: **sank, chipmunk, tanker** The letter n represents the /ng/ sound	**10. Oral Segmenting (Phoneme Fingers)** Say a word and the children use **Phoneme Fingers** to flick their fingers for each sound in: • p-i-n-k, s-a-n-k, ch-i-p-m-u-nk, t-a-nk-er The letter n represents the /ng/ sound

4. Manipulating (Swap) Sounds

Stick vowel cards at the top of the board: **a i**. Stick consonant cards at the bottom: **b r s th ng nk**

Play the **Full Circle Word Game** using the letters on the board to make a word. Ask the children to use **Phoneme Fingers** for each sound in the word. Read the word to the children. Ask a child to change one or more sounds in the word, swapping card/s from the word with card/s at either the bottom or the top of the board. Use **Phoneme Fingers** to make and read the new word. Continue the game changing one sound at a time until you get back to the first word made.

Full circle words: ink, think, thank, bank, bang, sang, rang, rank, rink, ink

5. Reading Words Ask children to read these words: • **pink, sank, chipmunk, tanker**	**11. Word Dictation** Ask children to tap for the sounds and write: • **pink, sank, chipmunk, tanker**
6. Reading Tricky Words: gone, goes For each word: • Show flashcard with the tricky bit underlined. • Together, with the children, sound and say the word using the known letter/sound matches. • Point out that the word doesn't sound like this, identify the tricky bit, and provide tricky sound: the 'n' in 'gone' sounds /n/; the 'es' in 'goes' sounds /z/. • Sound and say the word correctly together.	**12. Tricky Words Dictation: gone, goes** For each word: • Say the tricky word and remind children to watch out for the tricky bit. • Ask children to say the word, tap for the sounds and write each grapheme. Model with **Phoneme Fingers**, if necessary.
7. Reading Sentences (See page 139) The little girl had a pink dress. The boat sank in the open sea. The chipmunk had gone up the tree. The tanker goes to the port.	**13. Sentence Dictation** (See page 139) The little girl had a pink dress. The boat sank in the open sea. The chipmunk had gone up the tree. The tanker goes to the port. After writing, children read back sounds, words and sentences.

Look out for tricky word: little

Snappy Lesson 89

STEP 3.2

Sound /s/ written as s

Learning Objectives: to learn the main ways of spelling the sound /s/; to blend and segment words and sentences containing s

Success Criteria: to read words and sentences containing s spelling of sound /s/ and write dictated words and sentences with 100% accuracy

Reading	Spelling
1. Review Sounds (show as pack) • e ea ai ie nk	**7. Write Sounds** • e ea ai ie nk
2. Spelling: s Show the flashcard for **s**. Then with all the phonemes play the **Grab Game**. With the cards on the table, say a sound and ask the children to 'grab' for the letter. **Fingertips Freeze** when they touch the flashcard. Only allow one 'grab'.	**8. Spelling: s** Model writing the letter on the board and talk through letter formation. **Sky Write** the letter together. Ask children to write the sound on their whiteboards or paper. Check the letter formation for the correct start point, exit stroke and place on the line.
3. Oral Blending (Robot Game) Play the **Robot Game**. Pretend to be a Robot who can only speak in sounds (robot speech), moving arms back and forth like robot arms, in time with each sound. • Say the sounds **b-u-s**, ask children to listen and say the word. • Repeat for: **bus, nest, star, upset**	**9. Oral Segmenting (Phoneme Fingers)** Say a word and the children use **Phoneme Fingers** to flick their fingers for each sound in: • b-u-s, n-e-s-t, s-t-ar, u-p-s-e-t

4. Manipulating (Swap) Sounds

Stick vowel cards at the top of the board: **a o u**. Stick consonant cards at the bottom: **b g m p t s**

Play the **Full Circle Word Game** using the letters on the board to make a word. Ask the children to use **Phoneme Fingers** for each sound in the word. Read the word to the children. Ask a child to change one or more sounds in the word, swapping card/s from the word with card/s at either the bottom or the top of the board. Use **Phoneme Fingers** to make and read the new word. Continue the game changing one sound at a time until you get back to the first word made.

Full circle words: bus, gas, gap, gasp, spot, stop, stomp, stamp, tap, gap, gas, bus

5. Reading Words Ask children to read these words: • bus, nest, star, upset	**10. Word Dictation** Ask children to tap for the sounds and write: • bus, nest, star, upset
6. Reading Sentences (See page 139) The bus stops at the traffic lights. We found a bird's nest in the tree. Helen got a gold star for her story. Kim was upset about the bad news.	**11. Sentence Dictation** (See page 139) The bus stops at the traffic lights. We found a bird's nest in the tree. Helen got a gold star for her story. Kim was upset about the bad news. After writing, children read back sounds, words and sentences.

Snappy Lesson 90

STEP 3.2

Sound /s/ written as ss

Learning Objectives: to learn the main ways of spelling the sound /s/; to blend and segment words and sentences containing ss

Success Criteria: to read words and sentences containing ss spelling of sound /s/ and write dictated words and sentences with 100% accuracy

Reading	Spelling
1. Review Sounds (show as pack) • u ou o-e o nk s	**7. Write Sounds** • u ou o-e o nk s
2. New Spelling: ss Show the flashcard for **ss**. Then with all the phonemes play the **Grab Game**. With the cards on the table, say a sound and ask the children to 'grab' for the letter. **Fingertips Freeze** when they touch the flashcard. Only allow one 'grab'.	**8. New Spelling: ss** Model writing the letters on the board and talk through letter formation from exit stroke of first letter to start point of the next letter for joined-up writing. **Sky Write** the letters together. Ask children to write the sound on their whiteboards or paper. Check the letter formation for the correct start points, exit strokes and place on the line.
3. Oral Blending (Robot Game) Play the **Robot Game**. Pretend to be a Robot who can only speak in sounds (robot speech), moving arms back and forth like robot arms, in time with each sound. • Say the sounds **k-i-ss**, ask children to listen and say the word. • Repeat for: **dress, grass, class**	**9. Oral Segmenting (Phoneme Fingers)** Say a word and the children use **Phoneme Fingers** to flick their fingers for each sound in: • **k-i-ss, d-r-e-ss, g-r-a-ss, c-l-a-ss**

4. Manipulating (Swap) Sounds

Stick vowel cards at the top of the board: **a e i**
Stick consonant cards at the bottom: **c l m p t s ss**

Play the **Full Circle Word Game** using the letters on the board to make a word. Ask the children to use **Phoneme Fingers** for each sound in the word. Read the word to the children. Ask a child to change one or more sounds in the word, swapping card/s from the word with card/s at either the bottom or the top of the board. Use **Phoneme Fingers** to make and read the new word. Continue the game changing one sound at a time until you get back to the first word made.

Full circle words: clasp, class, lass, last, less, mess, miss, mist, list, lisp, clasp

5. Reading Words Ask children to read these words: • kiss, dress, grass, class	**10. Word Dictation** Ask children to tap for the sounds and write: • kiss, dress, grass, class
6. Reading Sentences (See page 139) Would you hug and kiss a cactus? Did you dress up as a cowboy? The grass grows tall in the meadow. There are thirty children in the class.	**11. Sentence Dictation** (See page 139) Would you hug and kiss a cactus? Did you dress up as a cowboy? The grass grows tall in the meadow. There are thirty children in the class. After writing, children read back sounds, words and sentences.

Snappy Lesson 91

STEP 3.2

Sound /s/ written as c(e) Letter c sounds /s/ when followed by the letter e

Learning Objectives: to learn the main ways of spelling the sound /s/; to blend and segment words and sentences containing c(e)

Success Criteria: to read words and sentences containing c(e) spelling of sound /s/ and write dictated words and sentences with 100% accuracy

General Note: /s/ is written as c(e) in words where the 'c' comes in the middle of a split digraph to create an /s/ sound, or where the 'e' is sounded.

Reading

1. Review Sounds (show as pack)
- nk s ss

2. New Spelling: c(e)
Show the flashcard for **c(e)**. Then with all the phonemes play the **Grab Game**. With the cards on the table, say a sound and ask the children to 'grab' for the letter. **Fingertips Freeze** when they touch the flashcard. Only allow one 'grab'.

3. Oral Blending (Robot Game)
Play the **Robot Game**. Pretend to be a Robot who can only speak in sounds (robot speech), moving arms back and forth like robot arms, in time with each sound.
- Say the sounds **(a-e)-c**, ask children to listen and say the word.
- Repeat for: **price, nice, success**

4. Manipulating (Swap) Sounds

Stick vowel cards at the top of the board: **i e a a-e ay**
Stick consonant cards at the bottom: **f h l m p r t s ss c**

Play the **Full Circle Word Game** using the letters on the board to make a word. Use two separate cards to make the split digraph a-e, ensuring children understand that this makes one sound. Ask the children to use **Phoneme Fingers** for each sound in the word. Read the word to the children. Ask a child to change one or more sounds in the word, swapping card/s from the word with card/s at either the bottom or the top of the board. Use **Phoneme Fingers** to make and read the new word. Continue the game changing one sound at a time until you get back to the first word made.

Full circle words: ace, space, pace, place, lace, face, race, trace, stray, say, hay, hiss, miss, mess, mass, ass, ace

5. Reading Words
Ask children to read these words:
- **ace, price, nice, success**

6. Reading Sentences (See page 140)
His highest card was an ace.
What is the price of the jacket?
Ben gave Chris a nice present.
Their success was due to their ability.

Spelling

7. Write Sounds
- nk s ss

8. New Spelling: c(e)
Model writing the letters on the board and talk through letter formation from exit stroke of first letter to start point of the next letter for joined-up writing. **Sky Write** the letters together. Ask children to write the sound on their whiteboards or paper. Check the letter formation for the correct start points, exit strokes and place on the line.

9. Oral Segmenting (Phoneme Fingers)
Say a word and the children use **Phoneme Fingers** to flick their fingers for each sound in:
- **(a-e)-c, p-r-(i-e)-c, n-(i-e)-c, s-u-c-c-e-ss**

10. Word Dictation
Ask children to tap for the sounds and write:
- **ace, price, nice, success**

11. Sentence Dictation (See page 140)
His highest card was an ace.
What is the price of the jacket?
Ben gave Chris a nice present.
Their success was due to their ability.

After writing, children read back sounds, words and sentences.

Snappy Lesson 92

STEP 3.2

Sound /s/ written as c(i) — Letter c sounds /s/ when followed by the letter i

Learning Objectives: to learn the main ways of spelling the sound /s/; to blend and segment words and sentences containing c(i)

Success Criteria: to read words and sentences containing c(i) spelling of sound /s/ and write dictated words and sentences with 100% accuracy

Reading	Spelling
1. Review Sounds (show as pack) • c k ck ch nk s ss c(e)	**8. Write Sounds** • c k ck ch nk s ss c(e)
2. New Spelling: c(i) Show the flashcard for **c(i)**. Then with all the phonemes play the **Grab Game**. With the cards on the table, say a sound and ask the children to 'grab' for the letter. **Fingertips Freeze** when they touch the flashcard. Only allow one 'grab'.	**9. New Spelling: c(i)** Model writing the letters on the board and talk through letter formation from exit stroke of first letter to start point of the next letter for joined-up writing. **Sky Write** the letters together. Ask children to write the sound on their whiteboards or paper. Check the letter formation for the correct start points, exit strokes and place on the line.
3. Oral Blending (Robot Game) Play the **Robot Game**. Pretend to be a Robot who can only speak in sounds (robot speech), moving arms back and forth like robot arms, in time with each sound. • Say the sounds **c-i-t-y**, ask children to listen and say the word. • Repeat for: **cinema, circus**	**10. Oral Segmenting (Phoneme Fingers)** Say a word and the children use **Phoneme Fingers** to flick their fingers for each sound in: • **c-i-t-y, c-i-n-e-m-a, c-ir-c-u-s**
4. Manipulating (Swap) Sounds Stick vowel cards at the top of the board: **a e i**. Stick consonant cards at the bottom: **l n p s ss c** Play the **Full Circle Word Game** using the letters on the board to make a word. Ask the children to use **Phoneme Fingers** for each sound in the word. Read the word to the children. Ask a child to change one or more sounds in the word, swapping card/s from the word with card/s at either the bottom or the top of the board. Use **Phoneme Fingers** to make and read the new word. Continue the game changing one sound at a time until you get back to the first word made. **Full circle words:** pencil, pens, lens, less, pass, pan, pen, pencil	
5. Reading Words Ask children to read these words: • **city, cinema, circus**	**11. Word Dictation** Ask children to tap for the sounds and write: • **city, cinema, circus**
6. Reading Tricky Words: cir<u>le</u> • Show flashcard with the tricky bit underlined. • Together, with the children, sound and say the word using the known letter/sound matches. • Point out that the word doesn't sound like this, identify the tricky bit, and provide tricky sound: the 'le' sounds /l/. • Sound and say the word correctly together.	**12. Tricky Words Dictation: cir<u>le</u>** • Say the tricky word and remind children to watch out for the tricky bit. • Ask children to say the word, tap for the sounds and write each grapheme. Model with **Phoneme Fingers**, if necessary.
7. Reading Sentences (See page 140) New York is a large city. We saw a good film at the cinema. The circus was completely sold out. The people stood round in a circle.	**13. Sentence Dictation** (See page 140) New York is a large city. We saw a good film at the cinema. The circus was completely sold out. The people stood round in a circle. After writing, children read back sounds, words and sentences.

Snappy Lesson 93

STEP 3.2

Sound /s/ written as c(y) Letter c sounds /s/ when followed by the letter y

Learning Objectives: to learn the main ways of spelling the sound /s/; to blend and segment words and sentences containing c(y)

Success Criteria: to read words and sentences containing c(y) spelling of sound /s/ and write dictated words and sentences with 100% accuracy

Reading	Spelling
1. Review Sounds (show as pack) • j g(e) g(i) g(y) ge dge nk s ss c(e) c(i)	**7. Write Sounds** • j g(e) g(i) g(y) ge dge nk s ss c(e) c(i)
2. New Spelling: c(y) Show the flashcard for **c(y)**. Then with all the phonemes play the **Grab Game**. With the cards on the table, say a sound and ask the children to 'grab' for the letter. **Fingertips Freeze** when they touch the flashcard. Only allow one 'grab'.	**8. New Spelling: c(y)** Model writing the letters on the board and talk through letter formation from exit stroke of first letter to start point of the next letter for joined-up writing. **Sky Write** the letters together. Ask children to write the sound on their whiteboards or paper. Check the letter formation for the correct start points, exit strokes and place on the line.
3. Oral Blending (Robot Game) Play the **Robot Game**. Pretend to be a Robot who can only speak in sounds (robot speech), moving arms back and forth like robot arms, in time with each sound. • Say the sounds **c-y-l-i-n-d-er**, ask children to listen and say the word. • Repeat for: **acid, Cyprus, fancy**	**9. Oral Segmenting (Phoneme Fingers)** Say a word and the children use **Phoneme Fingers** to flick their fingers for each sound in: • **c-y-l-i-n-d-er, a-c-i-d, C-y-p-r-u-s, f-a-n-c-y**
4. Manipulating (Swap) Sounds Stick vowel cards at the top of the board: **a e u i y er** Stick consonant cards at the bottom: **c d g n t s c f p r** Play the **Full Circle Word Game** using the letters on the board to make a word. Ask the children to use **Phoneme Fingers** for each sound in the word. Read the word to the children. Ask a child to change one or more sounds in the word, swapping card/s from the word with card/s at either the bottom or the top of the board. Use **Phoneme Fingers** to make and read the new word. Continue the game changing one sound at a time until you get back to the first word made. **Full circle words: icy, fancy, cyst, acid, cider, Cyprus, cyst, icy**	
5. Reading Words Ask children to read these words: • **cycling, cylinder, Cyprus, fancy**	**10. Word Dictation** Ask children to tap for the sounds and write: • **cycling, cylinder, Cyprus, fancy**
6. Reading Sentences (See page 140) The model is shaped like a cylinder. Jane went on holiday to Cyprus. Do you have a fancy dress costume?	**11. Sentence Dictation** (See page 140) The model is shaped like a cylinder. Jane went on holiday to Cyprus. Do you have a fancy dress costume? After writing, children read back sounds, words and sentences.

Look out for tricky word: their

Snappy Lesson 94

STEP 3.2

Sound /s/ written as ce

Learning Objectives: to learn the main ways of spelling the sound /s/; to blend and segment words and sentences containing ce

Success Criteria: to read words and sentences containing ce spelling of sound /s/ and write dictated words and sentences with 100% accuracy

General Note: /s/ is written as ce in words where the adjacent letters 'ce' make the /s/ sound and there is no split digraph.

Reading	Spelling
1. Review Sounds (show as pack) • ch tch nk s ss c(e) c(i) c(y)	**7. Write Sounds** • ch tch nk s ss c(e) c(i) c(y)
2. New Spelling: ce Show the flashcard for **ce**. Then with all the phonemes play the **Grab Game**. With the cards on the table, say a sound and ask the children to 'grab' for the letter. **Fingertips Freeze** when they touch the flashcard. Only allow one 'grab'.	**8. New Spelling: ce** Model writing the letters on the board and talk through letter formation from exit stroke of first letter to start point of the next letter for joined-up writing. **Sky Write** the letters together. Ask children to write the sound on their whiteboards or paper. Check the letter formation for the correct start points, exit strokes and place on the line.
3. Oral Blending (Robot Game) Play the **Robot Game**. Pretend to be a Robot who can only speak in sounds (robot speech), moving arms back and forth like robot arms, in time with each sound. • Say the sounds **ch-oi-ce**, ask children to listen and say the word. • Repeat for: **France, dance, peace**	**9. Oral Segmenting (Phoneme Fingers)** Say a word and the children use **Phoneme Fingers** to flick their fingers for each sound in: • **ch-oi-ce, F-r-a-n-ce, d-a-n-ce, p-ea-ce**

4. Manipulating (Swap) Sounds

Stick vowel cards at the top of the board: **a i u y a-e ir**
Stick consonant cards at the bottom: **b c f d m n p r t th s ss c ce**

Play the **Full Circle Word Game** using the letters on the board to make a word. Use two separate cards to make the split digraph a-e, ensuring children understand that this makes one sound. Ask the children to use **Phoneme Fingers** for each sound in the word. Read the word to the children. Ask a child to change one or more sounds in the word, swapping card/s from the word with card/s at either the bottom or the top of the board. Use **Phoneme Fingers** to make and read the new word. Continue the game changing one sound at a time until you get back to the first word made.

Full circle words: sin, since, mince, prince, prance, rancid, brace, race, face, fuss, bus, circus, cyst, Cynthia, sin

5. Reading Words Ask children to read these words: • choice, France, dance, peace	**10. Word Dictation** Ask children to tap for the sounds and write: • choice, France, dance, peace
6. Reading Sentences (See page 141) Did you make the right choice? Is Paris the capital of France? The quickstep is a kind of dance. Their country is at peace.	**11. Sentence Dictation** (See page 141) Did you make the right choice? Is Paris the capital of France? The quickstep is a kind of dance. Their country is at peace. After writing, children read back sounds, words and sentences.

Snappy Lesson 95

STEP 3.2

Sound /s/ written as se

Learning Objectives: to learn the main ways of spelling the sound /s/; to blend and segment words and sentences containing se

Success Criteria: to read words and sentences containing se spelling of sound /s/ and write dictated words and sentences with 100% accuracy

Reading	Spelling
1. Review Sounds (show as pack) • nk s ss c(e) c(i) c(y) ce	**7. Write Sounds** • nk s ss c(e) c(i) c(y) ce
2. New Spelling: se Show the flashcard for **se**. Then with all the phonemes play the **Grab Game**. With the cards on the table, say a sound and ask the children to 'grab' for the letter. **Fingertips Freeze** when they touch the flashcard. Only allow one 'grab'.	**8. New Spelling: se** Model writing the letters on the board and talk through letter formation from exit stroke of first letter to start point of the next letter for joined-up writing. **Sky Write** the letters together. Ask children to write the sound on their whiteboards or paper. Check the letter formation for the correct start points, exit strokes and place on the line.
3. Oral Blending (Robot Game) Play the **Robot Game**. Pretend to be a Robot who can only speak in sounds (robot speech), moving arms back and forth like robot arms, in time with each sound. • Say the sounds **l-oo-se**, ask children to listen and say the word. • Repeat for: **house, mouse, horse**	**9. Oral Segmenting (Phoneme Fingers)** Say a word and the children use **Phoneme Fingers** to flick their fingers for each sound in: • **l-oo-se, h-ou-se, m-ou-se, h-or-se**

4. Manipulating (Swap) Sounds

Stick vowel cards at the top of the board: **e oi ou ea**
Stick consonant cards at the bottom: **g h l m n p r v ch ss c ce se**

Play the **Full Circle Word Game** using the letters on the board to make a word. Ask the children to use **Phoneme Fingers** for each sound in the word. Read the word to the children. Ask a child to change one or more sounds in the word, swapping card/s from the word with card/s at either the bottom or the top of the board. Use **Phoneme Fingers** to make and read the new word. Continue the game changing one sound at a time until you get back to the first word made.

Full circle words: house, mouse, grouse, louse, lease, grease, lease, less, chess, choice, voice, peace, pounce, house

| **5. Reading Words**
Ask children to read these words:
• **loose, house, mouse, horse** | **10. Word Dictation**
Ask children to tap for the sounds and write:
• **loose, house, mouse, horse** |
| **6. Reading Sentences** (See page 141)
The screw is loose.
Do you live in a large house?
Can a mouse swim in water?
Have you ever seen a magic horse? | **11. Sentence Dictation** (See page 141)
The screw is loose.
Do you live in a large house?
Can a mouse swim in water?
Have you ever seen a magic horse?

After writing, children read back sounds, words and sentences. |

Snappy Lesson 96 *FastTrack*

STEP 3.2

Review: Sound /s/ written as s, ss, c(e), c(i), c(y), ce, se

Learning Objectives: to review a set of letter/sound correspondences; to learn the main ways of spelling the sound /s/, read these spelling choices in words and sentences and write them in dictated words and sentences.

Example grid:

s	ss	c(e)	c(i)	c(y)	ce	se
sat	less	ice	acid	icy	voice	house
sit	hiss	central	circle	cycle	peace	mouse
sun	mass	cent	circus	cyst	dance	horse
sell	mess	cell	pencil	cygnet	since	promise
sold	fuss	place	cider	racy	prince	please
gas	address	December	excite	Cynthia	office	because

1. Draw a blank seven-column grid on the board and explain that the group will be finding the main ways that the sound /s/ can be written down.

2. Show the flashcard for /s/ and ask children the main ways of writing the /s/ sound. They may use letter names. Write the graphemes at the top of the columns on the grid.

3. Ask the children to say a word that contains the sound /s/ and then to say which column it goes into. Write the choice in the correct column.

4. Ask the children to continue to generate examples while you write them in the correct column. There are some examples shown in the grid above if the children need prompting. Keep going until the columns are full.

5. Ask one child to come to the board, read the words in that column, underline the pattern, and comment on the position of the alternative spelling pattern in the word (i.e. beginning, middle or end).

6. Ask children to come to the board in turn until all of the alternative spelling patterns have been read, underlined and the position of the alternative spelling pattern commented on.

7. Children copy the grid into their books. Explain that they can add to this over time. Alternatively, make copies of the grid (see page 141) and stick these into the children's books. Explain that the words in this grid may not be exactly the same as those the children came up with.

8. Remove the grid from the board and dictate words (see example grid above) and the following sentences to the group for them to write down on a clean page or mini-whiteboard.

   There was a gas leak in the street.
   I made less mess than you did.
   Central Park will look magnificent in December.
   They were excited about going to the circus.
   Don't cycle on the icy path!
   The prince asked her to dance with him.
   Please get that mouse out of my house!

9. After writing the dictation, ask the children to read back a selection of words and sentences. Check for correct spelling choices and punctuation.

10. Ask the children to write a sentence of their own, using one of the words they have encountered. Listen to the children say the sentences aloud first. Moderate grammar and check for correct spelling choices and punctuation.

Snappy Lesson 97

STEP 3.2

Sound /w/ written as w

Learning Objectives: learn the main ways of spelling the sound /w/; to blend and segment words and sentences containing w

Success Criteria: to read words and sentences containing w spelling of sound /w/ and write dictated words and sentences with 100% accuracy

Reading	Spelling
1. Review Sounds (show as pack) • s ss c(e) c(i) c(y) ce se	**8. Write Sounds** • s ss c(e) c(i) c(y) ce se
2. Spelling: w Show the flashcard for **w**. Then with all the phonemes play the **Grab Game**. With the cards on the table, say a sound and ask the children to 'grab' for the letter. **Fingertips Freeze** when they touch the flashcard. Only allow one 'grab'.	**9. Spelling: w** Model writing the letter on the board and talk through letter formation. **Sky Write** the letter together. Ask children to write the sound on their whiteboards or paper. Check the letter formation for the correct start point, exit stroke and place on the line.
3. Oral Blending (Robot Game) Play the **Robot Game**. Pretend to be a Robot who can only speak in sounds (robot speech), moving arms back and forth like robot arms, in time with each sound. • Say the sounds **w-i-sh**, ask children to listen and say the word. • Repeat for: **twin, cobweb, wing**	**10. Oral Segmenting (Phoneme Fingers)** Say a word and the children use **Phoneme Fingers** to flick their fingers for each sound in: • w-i-sh, t-w-i-n, c-o-b-w-e-b, w-i-ng
4. Manipulating (Swap) Sounds Stick vowel card at the top of the board: **i**. Stick consonant cards at the bottom: **b g n s t t w** Play the **Full Circle Word Game** using the letters on the board to make a word. Ask the children to use **Phoneme Fingers** for each sound in the word. Read the word to the children. Ask a child to change one or more sounds in the word, swapping card/s from the word with card/s at either the bottom or the top of the board. Use **Phoneme Fingers** to make and read the new word. Continue the game changing one sound at a time until you get back to the first word made. **Full circle words: win, bin, bit, big, wig, twig, twist, twit, twin, win**	
5. Reading Words Ask children to read these words: • **wish, twin, cobweb, wing**	**11. Word Dictation** Ask children to tap for the sounds and write: • **wish, twin, cobweb, wing**
6. Reading Tricky Words: <u>pe</u>op<u>le</u> • Show flashcard with the tricky bits underlined. • Together, with the children, sound and say the word using the known letter/sound matches. • Point out that the word doesn't sound like this, identify the tricky bits, and provide tricky sounds: the 'eo' sounds /ee/ and the 'le' sounds /l/. • Sound and say the word correctly together.	**12. Tricky Words Dictation: <u>pe</u>op<u>le</u>** • Say the tricky word and remind children to watch out for the tricky bits. • Ask children to say the word, tap for the sounds and write each grapheme. Model with **Phoneme Fingers**, if necessary.
7. Reading Sentences (See page 142) The people wish they could dance. Do twins look the same as each other? Do spiders spin cobwebs? The magpie had a broken wing.	**13. Sentence Dictation** (See page 142) The people wish they could dance. Do twins look the same as each other? Do spiders spin cobwebs? The magpie had a broken wing. After writing, children read back sounds, words and sentences.

Snappy Lesson 98

STEP 3.2

Sound /w/ written as wh

Learning Objectives: learn the main ways of spelling the sound /w/; to blend and segment words and sentences containing wh

Success Criteria: to read words and sentences containing wh spelling of sound /w/ and write dictated words and sentences with 100% accuracy

General note: wh has an alternative pronunciation in some accents

Reading	Spelling
1. Review Sounds (show as pack) • s ss c(e) c(i) c(y) ce se w	**7. Write Sounds** • s ss c(e) c(i) c(y) ce se w
2. New Spelling: wh Show the flashcard for **wh**. Then with all the phonemes play the **Grab Game**. With the cards on the table, say a sound and ask the children to 'grab' for the letter. **Fingertips Freeze** when they touch the flashcard. Only allow one 'grab'.	**8. New Spelling: wh** Model writing the letters on the board and talk through letter formation from exit stroke of first letter to start point of the next letter for joined-up writing. **Sky Write** the letters together. Ask children to write the sound on their whiteboards or paper. Check the letter formation for the correct start points, exit strokes and place on the line.
3. Oral Blending (Robot Game) Play the **Robot Game**. Pretend to be a Robot who can only speak in sounds (robot speech), moving arms back and forth like robot arms, in time with each sound. • Say the sounds **wh-ee-l**, ask children to listen and say the word. • Repeat for: **whisper, white, which**	**9. Oral Segmenting (Phoneme Fingers)** Say a word and the children use **Phoneme Fingers** to flick their fingers for each sound in: • **wh-ee-l, wh-i-s-p-er, wh-(i-e)-t, wh-i-ch**
4. Manipulating (Swap) Sounds Stick vowel cards at the top of the board: **i ee a-e ea i-e** Stick consonant cards at the bottom: **t p f l w wh** Play the **Full Circle Word Game** using the letters on the board to make a word. Use two separate cards to make the split digraphs a-e and i-e, ensuring children understand that these make one sound. Ask the children to use **Phoneme Fingers** for each sound in the word. Read the word to the children. Ask a child to change one or more sounds in the word, swapping card/s from the word with card/s at either the bottom or the top of the board. Use **Phoneme Fingers** to make and read the new word. Continue the game changing one sound at a time until you get back to the first word made. **Full circle words: wit, whit, white, wipe, wife, while, whale, wheel, wheat, wit**	
5. Reading Words Ask children to read these words: • **wheel, whisper, white, which**	**10. Word Dictation** Ask children to tap for the sounds and write: • **wheel, whisper, white, which**
6. Reading Sentences (See page 142) The wheels of the bus went round. Can you speak up and not whisper? Is vanilla ice-cream white? Which book do you want to read?	**11. Sentence Dictation** (See page 142) The wheels of the bus went round. Can you speak up and not whisper? Is vanilla ice-cream white? Which book do you want to read? After writing, children read back sounds, words and sentences.

Snappy Lesson 99 *FastTrack*

STEP 3.2

Review: Sound /w/ written as w, wh

Learning Objectives: to review a set of letter/sound correspondences; to learn the main ways of spelling the sound /w/, read these spelling choices in words and sentences and write them in dictated words and sentences.

Example grid:

w	wh
will	when
wet	what
wind	which
wax	why
with	where
window	whenever

1. Draw a blank two-column grid on the board and explain that the group will be finding the main ways that the sound /w/ can be written down.

2. Show the flashcard for /w/ and ask children the main ways of writing the /w/ sound. They may use letter names. Write the graphemes at the top of the columns on the grid.

3. Ask the children to say a word that contains the sound /w/ and then to say which column it goes into. Write the choice in the correct column.

4. Ask the children to continue to generate examples while you write them in the correct column. There are some examples shown in the grid above if the children need prompting. Keep going until the columns are full.

5. Ask one child to come to the board, read the words in that column, underline the pattern, and comment on the position of the alternative spelling pattern in the word (i.e. beginning, middle or end).

6. Ask children to come to the board in turn until all of the alternative spelling patterns have been read, underlined and the position of the alternative spelling pattern commented on.

7. Children copy the grid into their books. Explain that they can add to this over time. Alternatively, make copies of the grid (see page 142) and stick these into the children's books. Explain that the words in this grid may not be exactly the same as those the children came up with.

8. Remove the grid from the board and dictate words (see example grid above) and the following sentences to the group for them to write down on a clean page or mini-whiteboard.

    Please will you shut the window?
    Why do you scream whenever you see a mouse?

9. After writing the dictation, ask the children to read back a selection of words and sentences. Check for correct spelling choices and punctuation.

10. Ask the children to write a sentence of their own, using one of the words they have encountered. Listen to the children say the sentences aloud first. Moderate grammar and check for correct spelling choices and punctuation.

Snappy Lesson 100

STEP 3.2

Sound /sh/ written as ch

Learning Objectives: to learn the main ways of spelling the sound /sh/; to blend and segment words and sentences containing ch

Success Criteria: to read words and sentences containing ch spelling of sound /sh/ and write dictated words and sentences with 100% accuracy

Reading	Spelling
1. Review Sounds (show as pack) • w wh	**7. Write Sounds** • w wh
2. New Spelling: ch If necessary, revise one of the /sh/ lessons from Teacher's Guide 2 Snappy Lessons 1-4, Step 2.1. Show the flashcard for **ch**. Then with all the phonemes play the **Grab Game**. With the cards on the table, say a sound and ask the children to 'grab' for the letter. **Fingertips Freeze** when they touch the flashcard. Only allow one 'grab'.	**8. New Spelling: ch** Model writing the letters on the board and talk through letter formation from exit stroke of first letter to start point of the next letter for joined-up writing. **Sky Write** the letters together. Ask children to write the sound on their whiteboards or paper. Check the letter formation for the correct start points, exit strokes and place on the line.
3. Oral Blending (Robot Game) Play the **Robot Game**. Pretend to be a Robot who can only speak in sounds (robot speech), moving arms back and forth like robot arms, in time with each sound. • Say the sounds **ch-e-f**, ask children to listen and say the word. • Repeat for: **chiffon, chevron, Chicago**	**9. Oral Segmenting (Phoneme Fingers)** Say a word and the children use **Phoneme Fingers** to flick their fingers for each sound in: • **ch-e-f, ch-iff-o-n, ch-e-v-r-o-n, Ch-i-c-a-g-o**

4. Manipulating (Swap) Sounds

Stick vowel cards at the top of the board: **e i o u-e**
Stick consonant cards at the bottom: **f ff t n r v ch**

Play the **Full Circle Word Game** using the letters on the board to make a word. Use two separate cards to make the split digraph u-e, ensuring children understand that this makes one sound. Ask the children to use **Phoneme Fingers** for each sound in the word. Read the word to the children. Ask a child to change one or more sounds in the word, swapping card/s from the word with card/s at either the bottom or the top of the board. Use **Phoneme Fingers** to make and read the new word. Continue the game changing one sound at a time until you get back to the first word made.

Full circle words: chef, chevron, chiffon, chute, chef

5. Reading Words Ask children to read these words: • **chef, chiffon, chevron, chute**	**10. Word Dictation** Ask children to tap for the sounds and write: • **chef, chiffon, chevron, chute**
6. Reading Sentences (See page 143) • **The chef cooks food in the canteen.** • **Charlene has a pink chiffon scarf.** • **Cars should keep two chevrons apart on the motorway.** • **Chandry slid down the chute into the swimming pool.**	**11. Sentence Dictation** (See page 143) • **The chef cooks food in the canteen.** • **Charlene has a pink chiffon scarf.** • **Cars should keep two chevrons apart on the motorway.** • **Chandry slid down the chute into the swimming pool.** After writing, children read back sounds, words and sentences.

Snappy Lesson 101

STEP 3.2

Sound /f/ written as f

Learning Objectives: to learn the main ways of spelling the sound /f/; to blend and segment words and sentences containing f

Success Criteria: read words and sentences with the main ways of spellings the sound /f/; write dictated /f/ words with 100% accuracy

Reading	Spelling
1. Review Sounds (show as pack) • w wh	**7. Write Sounds** • w wh
2. Spelling: f Show the flashcard for **f**. Then with all the phonemes play the **Grab Game**. With the cards on the table, say a sound and ask the children to 'grab' for the letter. **Fingertips Freeze** when they touch the flashcard. Only allow one 'grab'.	**8. Spelling: f** Model writing the letter on the board and talk through letter formation. **Sky Write** the letter together. Ask children to write the sound on their whiteboards or paper. Check the letter formation for the correct start point, exit stroke and place on the line.
3. Oral Blending (Robot Game) Play the **Robot Game**. Pretend to be a Robot who can only speak in sounds (robot speech), moving arms back and forth like robot arms, in time with each sound. • Say the sounds **f-u-n**, ask children to listen and say the word. • Repeat for: **fresh, fight, lift**	**9. Oral Segmenting (Phoneme Fingers)** Say a word and the children use **Phoneme Fingers** to flick their fingers for each sound in: • **f-u-n, f-r-e-sh, f-igh-t, l-i-f-t**

4. Manipulating (Swap) Sounds

Stick vowel cards at the top of the board: **e i ee ur ir**
Stick consonant cards at the bottom: **b d f s t th**

Play the **Full Circle Word Game** using the letters on the board to make a word. Ask the children to use **Phoneme Fingers** for each sound in the word. Read the word to the children. Ask a child to change one or more sounds in the word, swapping card/s from the word with card/s at either the bottom or the top of the board. Use **Phoneme Fingers** to make and read the new word. Continue the game changing one sound at a time until you get back to the first word made.

Full circle words: first, thirst, third, fir, fur, fee, bee, beef, tee, teeth, theft, fit, fist, first

5. Reading Words Ask children to read these words: • **fun, fresh, fight, lift**	**10. Word Dictation** Ask children to tap for the sounds and write: • **fun, fresh, fight, lift**
6. Reading Sentences (See page 143) Do you have fun at school? Fresh bread has a lovely smell. Once upon a time two giants had a fight. We took the lift to the hotel room.	**11. Sentence Dictation** (See page 143) Do you have fun at school? Fresh bread has a lovely smell. Once upon a time two giants had a fight. We took the lift to the hotel room. After writing, children read back sounds, words and sentences.

Look out for tricky word: once.

Snappy Lesson 102

STEP 3.1

Sound /f/ written as ff

Learning Objectives: to learn the main ways of spelling the sound /f/; to blend and segment words and sentences containing ff

Success Criteria: read words and sentences with the main ways of spellings the sound /f/; write dictated /f/ words with 100% accuracy

Reading	Spelling
1. Review Sounds (show as pack) • w wh f	**7. Write Sounds** • w wh f
2. New Spelling: ff Show the flashcard for **ff**. Then with all the phonemes play the **Grab Game**. With the cards on the table, say a sound and ask the children to 'grab' for the letter. **Fingertips Freeze** when they touch the flashcard. Only allow one 'grab'.	**8. New Spelling: ff** Model writing the letters on the board and talk through letter formation from exit stroke of first letter to start point of the next letter for joined-up writing. **Sky Write** the letters together. Ask children to write the sound on their whiteboards or paper. Check the letter formation for the correct start points, exit strokes and place on the line.
3. Oral Blending (Robot Game) Play the **Robot Game**. Pretend to be a Robot who can only speak in sounds (robot speech), moving arms back and forth like robot arms, in time with each sound. • Say the sounds **f-l-u-ff**, ask children to listen and say the word. • Repeat for: **sniff, stuffy, staffroom**	**9. Oral Segmenting (Phoneme Fingers)** Say a word and the children use **Phoneme Fingers** to flick their fingers for each sound in: • **f-l-u-ff, s-n-i-ff, s-t-u-ff-y, s-t-a-ff-r-oo-m**

4. Manipulating (Swap) Sounds (/ar sound)

Stick vowel cards at the top of the board: **a o u**. Stick consonant cards at the bottom: **c d h l p s t f ff**

Play the **Full Circle Word Game** using the letters on the board to make a word. Ask the children to use **Phoneme Fingers** for each sound in the word. Read the word to the children. Ask a child to change one or more sounds in the word, swapping card/s from the word with card/s at either the bottom or the top of the board. Use **Phoneme Fingers** to make and read the new word. Continue the game changing one sound at a time until you get back to the first word made.

Full circle words: of, off, puff, huff, cuff, stuff, staff, fluff, doff, off, of

5. Reading Words Ask children to read these words: • **fluff, sniff, stuffy, staffroom**	**10. Word Dictation** Ask children to tap for the sounds and write: • **fluff, sniff, stuffy, staffroom**
6. Reading Sentences (See page 143) Dad swept away the fluff with a brush. Please blow your nose and do not sniff. Too many rooms in the house are stuffy. All the teachers are in the staffroom.	**11. Sentence Dictation** (See page 143) Dad swept away the fluff with a brush. Please blow your nose and do not sniff. Too many rooms in the house are stuffy. All the teachers are in the staffroom. After writing, children read back sounds, words and sentences.

Look out for tricky word: please

Snappy Lesson 103

STEP 3.1

Sound /f/ written as ph

Learning Objectives: to learn the main ways of spelling the sound /f/; to blend and segment words and sentences containing ph

Success Criteria: read words and sentences with the main ways of spellings the sound /f/; write dictated /f/ words with 100% accuracy

Reading	Spelling
1. Review Sounds (show as pack) • w wh f ff	**7. Write Sounds** • w wh f ff
2. New Spelling: ph Show the flashcard for **ph**. Then with all the phonemes play the **Grab Game**. With the cards on the table, say a sound and ask the children to 'grab' for the letter. **Fingertips Freeze** when they touch the flashcard. Only allow one 'grab'.	**8. New Spelling: ph** Model writing the letters on the board and talk through letter formation from exit stroke of first letter to start point of the next letter for joined-up writing. **Sky Write** the letters together. Ask children to write the sound on their whiteboards or paper. Check the letter formation for the correct start points, exit strokes and place on the line.
3. Oral Blending (Robot Game) Play the **Robot Game**. Pretend to be a Robot who can only speak in sounds (robot speech), moving arms back and forth like robot arms, in time with each sound. • Say the sounds **d-o-l-ph-i-n**, ask children to listen and say the word. • Repeat for: **phantom, elephant, telephone**	**9. Oral Segmenting (Phoneme Fingers)** Say a word and the children use **Phoneme Fingers** to flick their fingers for each sound in: • **d-o-l-ph-i-n, ph-a-n-t-o-m, e-l-e-ph-a-n-t, t-e-l-e-ph-(o-e)-n**
4. Manipulating (Swap) Sounds Stick vowel cards at the top of the board: **a e i o** Stick consonant cards at the bottom: **d l ll m n t f ff ph** Play the **Full Circle Word Game** using the letters on the board to make a word. Ask the children to use **Phoneme Fingers** for each sound in the word. Read the word to the children. Ask a child to change one or more sounds in the word, swapping card/s from the word with card/s at either the bottom or the top of the board. Use **Phoneme Fingers** to make and read the new word. Continue the game changing one sound at a time until you get back to the first word made. **Full circle words: off, of, if, fill, Phil, fin, dolphin, phantom, fan, fen, fell, fill, if, of, off**	
5. Reading Words Ask children to read these words: • **dolphin, phantom, elephant, telephone**	**10. Word Dictation** Ask children to tap for the sounds and write: • **dolphin, phantom, elephant, telephone**
6. Reading Sentences (See page 144) In Florida we swam with the dolphins. The audience loved the Phantom of the Opera. There are no elephants in the zoo. Who was it on the telephone?	**11. Sentence Dictation** (See page 144) In Florida we swam with the dolphins. The audience loved the Phantom of the Opera. There are no elephants in the zoo. Who was it on the telephone? After writing, children read back sounds, words and sentences.

Snappy Lesson 104

STEP 3.1

Sound /f/ written as gh

Learning Objectives: to learn the main ways of spelling the sound /f/; to blend and segment words and sentences containing gh

Success Criteria: read words and sentences with the main ways of spellings the sound /f/; write dictated /f/ words with 100% accuracy

Reading	Spelling
1. Review Sounds (show as pack) • w wh f ff ph	**8. Write Sounds** • w wh f ff ph
2. New Spelling: gh Show the flashcard for **gh**. Then with all the phonemes play the **Grab Game**. With the cards on the table, say a sound and ask the children to 'grab' for the letter. **Fingertips Freeze** when they touch the flashcard. Only allow one 'grab'.	**9. New Spelling: gh** Model writing the letters on the board and talk through letter formation from exit stroke of first letter to start point of the next letter for joined-up writing. **Sky Write** the letters together. Ask children to write the sound on their whiteboards or paper. Check the letter formation for the correct start points, exit strokes and place on the line.
3. Oral Blending (Robot Game) Play the **Robot Game**. Pretend to be a Robot who can only speak in sounds (robot speech), moving arms back and forth like robot arms, in time with each sound. • Say the sounds **t-ou-gh**, ask children to listen and say the word. • Repeat for: **rough, enough**	**10. Oral Segmenting (Phoneme Fingers)** Say a word and the children use **Phoneme Fingers** to flick their fingers for each sound in: • **t-ou-gh, r-ou-gh, e-n-ou-gh**

4. Manipulating (Swap) Sounds

Stick vowel cards at the top of the board: **o u e o-e ou au**. Stick consonant cards at the bottom: **c n p r s t ff ph gh**

Play the **Full Circle Word Game** using the letters on the board to make a word. Use two separate cards to make the split digraph o-e, ensuring children understand that this makes one sound. Ask the children to use **Phoneme Fingers** for each sound in the word. Read the word to the children. Ask a child to change one or more sounds in the word, swapping card/s from the word with card/s at either the bottom or the top of the board. Use **Phoneme Fingers** to make and read the new word. Continue the game changing one sound at a time until you get back to the first word made.

Full circle words: tough, rough, rope, phone, stone, stuff, toff, off, cuff, rough, enough, tough

5. Reading Words Ask children to read these words: • **tough, rough, enough**	**11. Word Dictation** Ask children to tap for the sounds and write: • **tough, rough, enough**
6. Reading Tricky Words: laugh, cough For each word: • Show flashcard with the tricky bit underlined. • Together, with the children, sound and say the word using the known letter/sound matches. • Point out that the word doesn't sound like this, identify the tricky bit, and provide tricky sound: the 'au' in 'laugh' sounds /a/ or /ar/ depending on accent; the 'ou' in 'cough' sounds /o/. • Sound and say the word correctly together.	**12. Tricky Words Dictation: laugh, cough** For each word: • Say the tricky word and remind children to watch out for the tricky bit. • Ask children to say the word, tap for the sounds and write each grapheme. Model with **Phoneme Fingers**, if necessary.
7. Reading Sentences (See page 144) The tough stain would not come out. Last night the tramp slept rough. I think you have laughed enough. After his cold Chris had a bad cough.	**13. Sentence Dictation** (See page 144) The tough stain would not come out. Last night the tramp slept rough. I think you have laughed enough. After his cold Chris had a bad cough. After writing, children read back sounds, words and sentences.

Snappy Lesson 105 — FastTrack

STEP 3.2

Review: Sound /f/ written as f, ff, ph, gh

Learning Objectives: to review a set of letter/sound correspondences; to learn the main ways of spelling the sound /f/, read these spelling choices in words and sentences and write them in dictated words and sentences.

Example grid:

f	ff	ph	gh
if	off	Philip	rough
fuss	puff	telephone	tough
fit	huff	photograph	enough
fan	cuff	phonics	
fish	stuff	alphabet	
foil	staff	elephant	

1. Draw a blank four-column grid on the board and explain that the group will be finding the main ways that the sound /f/ can be written down.

2. Show the flashcard for /f/ and ask children the main ways of writing the /f/ sound. They may use letter names. Write the graphemes at the top of the columns on the grid.

3. Ask the children to say a word that contains the sound /f/ and then to say which column it goes into. Write the choice in the correct column.

4. Ask the children to continue to generate examples while you write them in the correct column. There are some examples shown in the grid above if the children need prompting. Keep going until the columns are full.

5. Ask one child to come to the board, read the words in that column, underline the pattern, and comment on the position of the alternative spelling pattern in the word (i.e. beginning, middle or end).

6. Ask children to come to the board in turn until all of the alternative spelling patterns have been read, underlined and the position of the alternative spelling pattern commented on.

7. Children copy the grid into their books. Explain that they can add to this over time. Alternatively, make copies of the grid (see page 144) and stick these into the children's books. Explain that the words in this grid may not be exactly the same as those the children came up with.

8. Remove the grid from the board and dictate words (see example grid above) and the following sentences to the group for them to write down on a clean page or mini-whiteboard.

    If I am late do not make a fuss.
    Whatever is that fluffy stuff on her cuffs?
    Philip took a photo of the elephant.
    Shark skin feels rough and tough.

9. After writing the dictation, ask the children to read back a selection of words and sentences. Check for correct spelling choices and punctuation.

10. Ask the children to write a sentence of their own, using one of the words they have encountered. Listen to the children say the sentences aloud first. Moderate grammar and check for correct spelling choices and punctuation.

Snappy Lesson 1

STEP 3.1

Sound /i/ written as i

He hit the nail with his hammer.
She had a cup of milk.
The tap has a drip.
You twist the jar once.

Snappy Lesson 2

STEP 3.1

Sound /i/ written as y

We visited the pyramids.
Atlantis is a myth.
The card was sympathetic.
The sprinter went to the Olympics.

Snappy Lesson 3

STEP 3.1

Review: Sound /i/ written as i, y

i	y
pin	myth
sit	crystal
limp	sympathetic
wind	pyramid
slip	Olympics
wish	

Snappy Lesson 4

STEP 3.1

Sound /ai/ written as ai

She put a nail in the pail.
I shall aim at the target.
Can the boat sail to Scotland?
There was a stain on the carpet.

Snappy Lesson 5

STEP 3.1

Sound /ai/ written as a-e

Josh went on a date with Liz.
She put the cake in a tin.
The car got stuck in the lane.
We had a good game of tennis.

Snappy Lesson 6

STEP 3.1

Sound /ai/ written as ay

Push the hay into the pen.
The coins lay deep in the soil.
He fed the stray cat.
We will pray at school.

Snappy Lesson 7

STEP 3.1

Sound /ai/ written as ey

| The shark ate its prey. |
| They had to pull on the chain. |
| Her coat was grey with a red trim. |
| I will obey my mum. |

Snappy Lesson 8

STEP 3.1

Sound /ai/ written as a

| The baby slept in his pram. |
| The spring bulbs came up in April. |
| Is the house vacant? |
| Did the paper bag split? |

Snappy Lesson 9

STEP 3.1

Review: Sound /ai/ written as ai, a-e, ay, ey, a

ai	a-e	ay	ey	a
rain	made	day	they	paper
main	came	say	grey	acorn
rail	make	may	prey	bacon
wait	late	lay	obey	bagel
train	same	play		apricot
snail	snake	clay		

Snappy Lesson 10

STEP 3.1

Sound /ee/ written as ee

| Keep her safe from harm. |
| The bee stung me on the hand. |
| Come and meet his sister. |
| There are seven days in a week. |

Snappy Lesson 11

STEP 3.1

Sound /ee/ written as ea

| Please keep her safe from harm. |
| Take a seat in the waiting room. |
| A leaf fell from the tree. |
| A cup of tea is such a treat. |

Snappy Lesson 12

STEP 3.1

Sound /ee/ written as e

| They let me win. |
| Will the lemon tart be hot? |
| Did he go fishing? |
| Can she visit her children? |

Snappy Lesson 13

STEP 3.1

Sound /ee/ written as e-e

| They visited a theme park. |
| Will you help me pack these things? |
| I need to complete the test. |
| You must avoid extreme heat. |

Snappy Lesson 14

STEP 3.1

Sound /ee/ written as y

| The model has a slim body. |
| "I am happy," said Danny. |
| Will you explain the mystery? |
| The sympathy card was sad. |

Snappy Lesson 15

STEP 3.1

Sound /ee/ written as ie

| The thief was sent to jail. |
| Can umbrellas shield us from the sun? |
| The sheep ate the grass in the field. |
| The priest has a strong belief. |

Snappy Lesson 16 *FastTrack*

STEP 3.1

Review: Sound /ee/ written as ee, ea, e, e-e, y, ie

ee	ea	e	e-e	y	ie
see	eat	he	these	body	thief
feel	tea	me	eve	copy	brief
feet	read	she	theme	dusty	chief
need	team	we	complete	happy	field
tree	speak	be	extreme	baby	shriek
sheep	cream	frequent		very	

Snappy Lesson 17

STEP 3.1

Sound /ie/ written as ie

We can bake a great pie for supper.
Can you tie things up with string?
He tries to cut the meat.
The baby cries in the morning.

Snappy Lesson 18

STEP 3.1

Sound /ie/ written as i-e

They like to come for tea.
It's time for bed.
She will invite him to the party.
The children play outside.

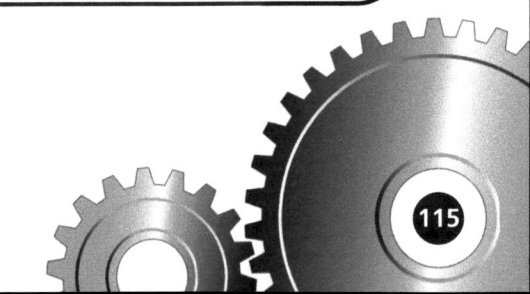

Snappy Lesson 19

STEP 3.1

Sound /ie/ written as igh

| Did Shane get a high mark? |
| Bob gave a loud sigh. |
| The garden light helps us to see. |
| It is dark at night. |

Snappy Lesson 20

STEP 3.1

Sound /ie/ written as y

| The train stops by the sea. |
| There are fish in my pond. |
| An umbrella keeps you dry. |
| The sun shines in the sky. |

Snappy Lesson 21

STEP 3.1

Sound /ie/ written as i

| The milkman left a pint of milk. |
| The child tried to float in the sea. |
| You remind me of the queen. |
| The moon went behind the cloud. |

Snappy Lesson 22 *FastTrack*

STEP 3.1

Review: Sound /ie/ written as ie, i-e, igh, y, i

ie	i-e	igh	y	i
pie	like	high	by	mind
lie	time	light	my	find
tie	ride	night	try	wild
cried	bike	fight	sky	kind
tried	shine	bright	deny	child
fried	prize	tonight	reply	blind

Snappy Lesson 23

STEP 3.1

Sound /oa/ written as oa

Is this wood oak or beech?
Joan went for an eye test.
The coach went round the corner.
He put the toast on a plate.

Snappy Lesson 24

STEP 3.1

Sound /oa/ written as o-e

Was there a flag on the pole?
They woke at three in the morning.
The note invited him to the party.
I put the letter in an envelope.

Snappy Lesson 25

STEP 3.1

Sound /oa/ written as o

| Please go away. |
| He kept gold bars in his safe. |
| Are you cold? |
| Both sisters were ill. |

Snappy Lesson 26

STEP 3.1

Sound /oa/ written as ow

| The torch glows with a bright light. |
| Will the wind blow out the flame? |
| The snow lies on the ground. |
| Show me your bike. |

Snappy Lesson 27

STEP 3.1

Sound /oa/ written as ou

| I can smell mould in the damp room. |
| Charlie was the life and soul of the party. |
| The farmer kept poultry in the back yard. |
| The ashes began to smoulder. |

Snappy Lesson 28 — FastTrack

STEP 3.1

Review: Sound /oa/ written as oa, o-e, o, ow, ou

oa	o-e	o	ow	ou
coat	home	no	low	soul
goat	hope	so	grow	mouldy
road	nose	go	snow	shoulder
foal	those	old	slow	boulder
boast	spoke	don't	window	
float	stone	most	yellow	

Snappy Lesson 29

STEP 3.1

Sound /ue/ written as ue

The bar was the venue for the quiz.
Were the bananas good value?
When was the statue painted?
The rescue party found the child.

Snappy Lesson 30

STEP 3.1

Sound /ue/ written as u-e

Is there a fuse in the plug?
Six of the shapes were cubes.
The tube of toothpaste was empty.
The farmer rode a mule to market.

Snappy Lesson 31

STEP 3.1

Sound /ue/ written as u

She plays the tuba.
The teacher was on duty.
Is a unicorn a real animal?
His uniform is too big.

Snappy Lesson 32

STEP 3.1

Sound /ue/ written as ew

The grass was wet with dew.
We sat in the chapel pew.
The cook made a rabbit stew.
I need to renew my book.

Snappy Lesson 33 *FastTrack*

STEP 3.1

Review: Sound /ue/ written as ue, u-e, u, ew

ue	u-e	u	ew
cue	use	pupil	few
due	cube	tuna	new
argue	tune	tulip	stew
rescue	tube	music	knew
statue	confuse	human	mildew
continue	computer	stupid	

Snappy Lesson 34

STEP 3.1

Sound /ar/ written as ar

The jar stood on the shelf.
Is the sun far away?
The bus went under the arch.
Where is the carpet?

Snappy Lesson 35

STEP 3.1

Sound /ar/ written as a

At last the lights came on.
The pie was rather tasty.
Father likes sweet things.
This soap makes a good lather.

Snappy Lesson 36 *FastTrack*

STEP 3.1

Review: Sound /ar/ written as ar, a

ar	a
bar	Father
car	rather
arm	fast
park	bath
card	last
start	grass
	class

Snappy Lesson 37

STEP 3.1

Sound /er/ written as er

| The queen has lots of servants. |
| They were late for dinner. |
| He hit the nail with his hammer. |
| Though we go away in the Summer, we like to have a winter holiday. |

Snappy Lesson 38

STEP 3.1

Sound /er/ written as ur

| The sheep hurt its foot. |
| Can a snake burp? |
| The pig has a curly tail. |
| Do you like Thursdays? |

Snappy Lesson 39

STEP 3.1

Sound /er/ written as ir

| Can a goat give birth to piglets? |
| The skirt was too long. |
| Jogging makes me thirsty. |
| Is thirteen a lucky number? |

Snappy Lesson 40 *FastTrack*

STEP 3.1

Review: Sound /er/ written as er, ur, ir

er	ur	ir
her	fur	girl
fern	burn	bird
term	turn	sir
herd	urn	shirt
herbs	hurt	third
stern	surf	first

Snappy Lesson 41

STEP 3.1

Sound /or/ written as or

Pork comes from a pig.
Do tulips have thorns?
A north wind is cold.
Her fur coat was short.

Snappy Lesson 42

STEP 3.1

Sound /or/ written as au

The crash was not my fault.
The wizard stirs his cauldron.
I might visit you in August.
Harvest supper is held in autumn.

Snappy Lesson 43

STEP 3.1

Sound /or/ written as aw

I tried not to yawn.
Is prawn salad on the menu?
The foal lay on dry straw.
She found her card in the drawer.

Snappy Lesson 44

STEP 3.1

Sound /or/ written as al

The stone wall is five feet high.
The fall hurt his leg.
The small kitten is cute.
Do you like to play football?

Snappy Lesson 45 *FastTrack*

STEP 3.1

Review: Sound /or/ written as or, au, aw, al

or	au	aw	al
for	Paul	saw	all
fork	haul	paw	ball
sort	launch	raw	talk
horse	haunted	jaw	walk
storm	August	law	call
forbid	automatic	shawl	beanstalk

Snappy Lesson 46

STEP 3.1

Sound /oi/ written as oi

The snake looks like a coil of rope.
A dart has a sharp point.
Will garlic spoil the taste of cake again?
Is the beef moist or dry?

Snappy Lesson 47

STEP 3.1

Sound /oi/ written as oy

The children broke the toy.
The boy plays outside.
Loud sounds annoy us.
Locusts can destroy crops.

Snappy Lesson 48 *FastTrack*

STEP 3.1

Review: Sound /oi/ written as oi, oy

oi	oy
oil	boy
boil	toy
coins	joy
join	oyster
soil	royal
moist	enjoy

Snappy Lesson 49

STEP 3.1

Sound /ou/ written as ou

| The sun went behind a cloud. |
| The teacher was proud of her class. |
| Turn round and look this way. |
| There is no need to shout. |

Snappy Lesson 50

STEP 3.1

Sound /ou/ written as ow

| The farmer keeps cows and horses. |
| Gran took a bus to the town. |
| The clown had a sad mouth. |
| Shall I paint the wall brown? |

Snappy Lesson 51 *FastTrack*

STEP 3.1

Review: Sound /ou/ written as ou, ow

ou	ow
out	now
about	down
cloud	owl
found	cow
ground	how
loudest	town

Snappy Lesson 52

STEP 3.1 .1

Sound /oo/ written as oo

I've looked for my coat.

I need to find the book.

Can you chop wood with a spade?

We get wool from sheep.

Snappy Lesson 53

STEP 3.1

Sound /oo/ written as oul

Would you like a cup of tea?

Could you come to my party?

I should try harder.

Snappy Lesson 54

STEP 3.1

Sound /oo/ written as u

He put on his shirt.

Help me push the pram.

You need to pull out the weeds.

The puppy is playful.

Snappy Lesson 55 *FastTrack*

STEP 3.1

Review: Sound /oo/ written as oo, oul, u

oo	oul	u
look	could	put
foot	would	pull
cook	should	push
good		full
book		bush
stood		playful

Snappy Lesson 56

STEP 3.1

Sound /oo/ written as oo

I had too much to eat.
A cloud went across the moon.
The roof needs new tiles.
What will cool you down?

Snappy Lesson 57

STEP 3.1

Sound /oo/ written as ue

He drives a light blue car.
Is it true she came late?
Glue can be very sticky.
I don't have a clue.

Snappy Lesson 58

STEP 3.1

Sound /oo/ written as ew

- The ship's crew became ill.
- Paul threw out the rubbish.
- We flew in a helicopter.
- Brew the tea in this teapot.

Snappy Lesson 59

STEP 3.1

Sound /oo/ written as u-e

- Luke burnt the toast.
- Kay eats prunes with her cornflakes.
- A plume of smoke came from the tower.
- If Roy wins, it will be a fluke.

Snappy Lesson 60

STEP 3.1

Sound /oo/ written as ou

- Have you ever been to Africa?
- Steve will open a tin of soup.
- The group of children went out.
- Amy got free sweets with the coupon.

Snappy Lesson 61

STEP 3.1

Sound /oo/ written as o

They are flying to Canada by plane.
Do the houses have outside lights?
The boxes fit into the case.
Can Pete come for supper tonight?

Snappy Lesson 62 *FastTrack*

STEP 3.1

Review: Sound /oo/ written as oo, ue, ew, u-e, ou, o

oo	ue	ew	u-e	ou	o
too	clue	blew	June	you	do
zoo	blue	chew	flute	soup	to
boot	glue	grew	rude	group	into
food	true	drew	rule		today
soon	Sue	flew	brute		
spoon	tissue	screw	conclude		

Snappy Lesson 63

STEP 3.1

Sound /e/ written as e

Bob has three pets at home.
Did you go to bed late?
The men took their bags.
Sally put up a shelf.

Snappy Lesson 64

STEP 3.1

Sound /e/ written as ea

> I like to toast my bread.
>
> Let us sail full speed ahead.
>
> The plane is ready for take-off.
>
> Stan had fried bacon for breakfast.

Snappy Lesson 65

STEP 3.1

Sound /e/ written as ai

> He said we had to pay.
>
> The car ran out of oil again.
>
> The desk stood against the wall.
>
> What you said can't be unsaid.

Snappy Lesson 66

STEP 3.1

Sound /e/ written as ie

> My friend Molly has a yellow kite.
>
> They have a strong friendship.
>
> The new teacher seems friendly.
>
> Wild dogs are unfriendly.

Snappy Lesson 67 FastTrack

STEP 3.1

Review: Sound /e/ written as e, ea, ai, ie

e	ea	ai	ie
get	head	said	friend
bed	dead	again	friendship
men	deaf	against	unfriendly
then	ready	unsaid	
neck	bread		
spend	instead		

Snappy Lesson 68

STEP 3.1

Sound /u/ written as u

We have hot cross buns at Easter.
The baby sat up in her pram.
Do you go home for lunch?
Mr and Mrs Smith found a coin under the tree.

Snappy Lesson 69

STEP 3.1

Sound /u/ written as ou

Steve is too young to join the army.
You can look but not touch.
Her cousin's name is Jane.
The president is famous.

Snappy Lesson 70

STEP 3.1

Sound /u/ written as o-e

| What has Jack done to the bike? |
| Would you like some cake? |
| When can Sue come to visit me? |
| I love to see tulips in bloom. |

Snappy Lesson 71

STEP 3.1

Sound /u/ written as o

| My son is a teacher. |
| The month of March was windy. |
| Her mother likes flowers. |
| His brother looks like him. |

Snappy Lesson 72 *FastTrack*

STEP 3.1

Review: Sound /u/ written as u, ou, o-e, o

u	ou	o-e	o
up	young	some	son
mum	cousin	come	front
run	touch	done	month
cup	country	love	mother
bus	famous	honey	brother
sunset	trouble	money	discover

Snappy Lesson 73

STEP 3.2

Sound /c/ written as c

Can you meet me in town?
The miners found coal in the mine.
He was hurt in a train crash.
We went for a picnic by the river.

Snappy Lesson 74

STEP 3.2

Sound /c/ written as k

The king sat on his throne.
Andrew put on his silk tie.
Sue has a dry skin.
Is her desk in the study?

Snappy Lesson 75

STEP 3.2

Sound /c/ written as ck

The duck laid five eggs.
Mother's neck became red in the sun.
Sweet things can make you sick.
These boys like to play on the rock.

Snappy Lesson 76

STEP 3.2

Sound /c/ written as ch

The school opens in the morning.
They all sing the chorus.
Can you explain the technical details?
The chemist closes at night.

Snappy Lesson 77 *FastTrack*

STEP 3.2

Review: Sound /c/ written as c, k, ck, ch

c	k	ck	ch
can	kid	kick	school
cot	king	sock	Christmas
clog	keep	sack	chemist
crust	milk	stuck	chronic
coal	skip	pocket	chemical
cling	soak	ticket	headache

Snappy Lesson 78

STEP 3.2

Sound /j/ written as j

Prue lost her job at the bakers.
Did you finish the apricot jam?
The jail is now full.
Did you enjoy it a little?

Snappy Lesson 79

STEP 3.2

Sound /j/ written as g(e)

- You are a gem.
- The gel came out of a tube.
- My pet gerbil was in a box.
- Hot coals generate heat.

Snappy Lesson 80

STEP 3.2

Sound /j/ written as g(i)

- Jack has a box of magic tricks.
- Kate read a story about a giant.
- Have you seen Patrick's ginger cat?
- I will draw a margin on the paper.

Snappy Lesson 81

STEP 3.2

Sound /j/ written as g(y)

- Gym club meets after school.
- The puppy has too much energy.
- They went to Egypt on holiday.
- The gypsy caravan is painted yellow.

Snappy Lesson 82

STEP 3.2

Sound /j/ written as ge

| My brother's name is George. |
| Coal was transported by barge. |
| Nathan has gone to college. |
| The Avon Gorge is in Bristol. |

Snappy Lesson 83

STEP 3.2

Sound /j/ written as dge

| The bridge goes over the river. |
| He has a badge on his uniform. |
| Can Judith give Dylan a nudge? |
| The gardener cut the hedge. |

Snappy Lesson 84 *FastTrack*

STEP 3.2

Review: Sound /j/ written as j, g(e), g(i), g(y), ge, dge

j	g(e)	g(i)	g(y)	ge	dge
jam	gel	gin	gym	age	fudge
jet	gem	magic	gymnast	page	hedge
jig	gent	ginger	gypsy	sausage	ridge
jog	agent	giraffe	Egypt	George	ledge
join	gently	giblets	energy	barge	badge
jacket	danger	giant	synergy	college	badger

Snappy Lesson 85

STEP 3.2

Sound /ch/ written as ch

I want fish and chips for tea.
We have lunch at one o'clock.
They took the coach to London.
The chicken must have some water.

Snappy Lesson 86

STEP 3.2

Sound /ch/ written as tch

Chris rode his bike into a ditch.
Did the cat scratch your hand?
The football match is on Saturday.
The garden gate has a latch.

Snappy Lesson 87 *FastTrack*

STEP 3.2

Review: Sound /ch/ written as ch, tch

ch	tch
chop	catch
chin	fetch
chug	notch
check	stitch
such	match
March	kitchen

Snappy Lesson 88

STEP 3.2

Sounds /ng+k/ written as nk

| The little girl had a pink dress. |
| The boat sank in the open sea. |
| The chipmunk had gone up the tree. |
| The tanker goes to the port. |

Snappy Lesson 89

STEP 3.2

Sound /s/ written as s

| The bus stops at the traffic lights. |
| We found a bird's nest in the tree. |
| Helen got a gold star for her story. |
| Kim was upset about the bad news. |

Snappy Lesson 90

STEP 3.2

Sound /s/ written as ss

| Would you hug and kiss a cactus? |
| Did you dress up as a cowboy? |
| The grass grows tall in the meadow. |
| There are thirty children in the class. |

Snappy Lesson 91

STEP 3.2

Sound /s/ written as c(e)

| His highest card was an ace. |
| What is the price of the jacket? |
| Ben gave Chris a nice present. |
| Their success was due to their ability. |

Snappy Lesson 92

STEP 3.2

Sound /s/ written as c(i)

| New York is a large city. |
| We saw a good film at the cinema. |
| The circus was completely sold out. |
| The people stood round in a circle. |

Snappy Lesson 93

STEP 3.2

Sound /s/ written as c(y)

| The model is shaped like a cylinder. |
| Jane went on holiday to Cyprus. |
| Do you have a fancy dress costume? |

Snappy Lesson 94

STEP 3.2

Sound /s/ written as ce

Did you make the right choice?
Is Paris the capital of France?
The quickstep is a kind of dance.
Their country is at peace.

Snappy Lesson 95

STEP 3.2

Sound /s/ written as se

The screw is loose.
Do you live in a large house?
Can a mouse swim in water?
Have you ever seen a magic horse?

Snappy Lesson 96 *FastTrack*

STEP 3.2

Review: Sound /s/ written as s, ss, c(e), c(i), c(y), ce, se

s	ss	c(e)	c(i)	c(y)	ce	se
sat	less	ice	acid	icy	voice	house
sit	hiss	central	circle	cycle	peace	mouse
sun	mass	cent	circus	cyst	dance	horse
sell	mess	cell	pencil	cygnet	since	promise
sold	fuss	place	cider	racy	prince	please
gas	address	December	excite	Cynthia	office	because

Snappy Lesson 97

STEP 3.2

Sound /w/ written as w

The people wish they could dance.
Do twins look the same as each other?
Do spiders spin cobwebs?
The magpie had a broken wing.

Snappy Lesson 98

STEP 3.2

Sound /w/ written as wh

The wheels of the bus went round.
Can you speak up and not whisper?
Is vanilla ice-cream white?
Which book do you want to read?

Snappy Lesson 99 *FastTrack*

STEP 3.2

Review: Sound /w/ written as w, wh

w	wh
will	when
wet	what
wind	which
wax	why
with	where
window	whenever

Snappy Lesson 100

STEP 3.2

Sound /sh/ written as ch

| The chef cooks food in the canteen. |
| Charlene has a pink chiffon scarf. |
| Cars should keep two chevrons apart on the motorway. |
| Chandry slid down the chute into the swimming pool. |

Snappy Lesson 101

STEP 3.2

Sound /f/ written as f

| Do you have fun at school? |
| Fresh bread has a lovely smell. |
| Once upon a time two giants had a fight. |
| We took the lift to the hotel room. |

Snappy Lesson 102

STEP 3.2

Sound /f/ written as ff

| Dad swept away the fluff with a brush. |
| Please blow your nose and do not sniff. |
| Too many rooms in the house are stuffy. |
| All the teachers are in the staffroom. |

Snappy Lesson 103

STEP 3.2

Sound /f/ written as ph

In Florida we swam with the dolphins.
The audience loved the Phantom of the Opera.
There are no elephants in the zoo.
Who was it on the telephone?

Snappy Lesson 104

STEP 3.2

Sound /f/ written as gh

The tough stain would not come out.
Last night the tramp slept rough.
I think you have laughed enough.
After his cold Chris had a bad cough.

Snappy Lesson 105 *FastTrack*

STEP 3.2

Review: Sound /f/ written as f, ff, ph, gh

f	ff	ph	gh
if	off	Philip	rough
fuss	puff	telephone	tough
fit	huff	photograph	enough
fan	cuff	phonics	
fish	stuff	alphabet	
foil	staff	elephant